4-4-73

BRITISH LABOUR STRUGGLES:
CONTEMPORARY PAMPHLETS 1727-1850

PRELUDE TO VICTORY

OF

THE TEN HOURS MOVEMENT

Two Speeches, One Letter
and a Report

1844

Arno Press

A New York Times Company/New York 1972

Reprint Edition 1972 by Arno Press Inc.

Reprinted from copies in the Kress Library
Graduate School of Business Administration,
Harvard University

BRITISH LABOUR STRUGGLES: CONTEMPORARY PAMPHLETS 1727-1850
ISBN for complete set: 0-405-04410-0

See last pages for complete listing.

Manufactured in the United States of America

Library of Congress Cataloging in Publication Data
Main entry under title:

Prelude to victory of the ten hours movement.

     (British labour struggles:
contemporary pamphlets 1727-1850)
     CONTENTS: A letter to Lord Ashley, on the principles
which regulate wages, by R. Torrens [first published
1844].--Ten hours' factory bill. The speech of Lord
Ashley in the House of Commons, on Friday, March 15th,
1844 [first published 1844].--Ten hours factory bill.
The speech of Lord Ashley in the House of Commons on
Friday, 10th May, 1844 [first published 1844]. [etc.]
     1. Hours of labor--Great Britain. 2. Factory laws
and legislation--Great Britain. 3. Factory system--
Great Britain. I. Series.
HD5166.P74   331.2'572   72-2536
ISBN 0-405-04429-1

1744934

Contents

A LETTER

TO

LORD ASHLEY,

ON THE

PRINCIPLES WHICH REGULATE WAGES

AND

ON THE MANNER AND DEGREE

IN WHICH

WAGES WOULD BE REDUCED,

BY THE PASSING OF

A TEN HOURS BILL.

By R. TORRENS, Esq., F.R.S.

LONDON:
SMITH, ELDER, AND CO., CORNHILL.
1844.

Price Two Shillings.

CONTENTS.

A

LETTER TO LORD ASHLEY,

&c.   &c.   &c.

My Lord,

THE principles which regulate the wages of labour form, without any exception, the most interesting and the most important division of Political Economy. The labouring classes compose the great bulk of every community; and a country is happy or miserable, as they are well or ill supplied with the necessaries, comforts, and enjoyments of life. The study of political economy, if it did not teach the way in which labour may obtain an adequate reward, might serve to gratify a merely speculative curiosity, but could scarcely conduce to any purposes of practical utility. It claims the peculiar attention of the benevolent and good, mainly because it explains the causes which depress and elevate wages, and thereby points out the means by which we may mitigate the distress and improve the condition of the great majority of mankind. Political economy is not, as has been erroneously stated, the appropriate science of the statesman and the legislator; it is peculiarly and emphatically *the science of the people.*

The Maximum of Wages.

As wages are paid out of the produce of industry, it is obvious that there are natural and necessary limits, beyond

B

which they cannot be permanently increased. Thus, if 100 labourers expend 200 quarters of corn for seed and implements, and raise a return of 500 quarters, it is physically impossible that their wages should continue to be more than 300 quarters; because if they did, seed and implements would not be replaced, and the capitalists could not continue the cultivation of the earth. Again, if it were necessary to resort to an inferior soil, upon which 100 labourers, with an expenditure of 200 quarters for seed and implements, could raise no more than 400 quarters, then, for the same reason, it would become physically impossible that the annual wages of 100 men should exceed 200 quarters of corn.

In the above cases the labourer is supposed to receive as his wages the whole produce of labour, which remains after the replacement of the capitalist's other advances. This can occur only in those rare instances in which the capitalist, without seeking any profit for himself, employs labourers from pure benevolence and charity. In the vast majority of actual cases, the capitalist, in addition to the replacement of all his advances, will reserve a portion of the produce of industry as his profit; and though there will exist no physical, yet there will be a moral impossibility that wages should exceed that which remains after the capitalist's other advances have been replaced, with the lowest rate of increase, for the sake of which he will carry on his business. This, then, we may call the *moral maximum* of wages. The labourer may receive more, as a benevolent gift, from men of fortune, who do not live upon their industry; but he cannot receive more, in exchange for common labour, in those great and permanent branches of employment which supply the community with the necessaries and comforts of life.

The rate of increase, which is sufficient to induce the capitalist to continue in business, varies from causes which it is not necessary here to explain. We may for the present

safely assume that the capitalist will not engage in the work
of production, unless he can obtain a profit of 7 per cent.

If we take 7 per cent. as the lowest rate of profit, then
the maximum, beyond which wages cannot rise, will be that
portion of the produce which remains, after replacing the
advances not consisting of wages, and deducting what is
equivalent to 7 per cent. upon the whole advances. Thus,
if a farmer advance to 100 labourers 200 quarters of corn
as wages, with 200 quarters more for seed and implements;
and if he obtain a return of 428 quarters, wages will be at
the maximum, for if we take from the whole produce of 428
quarters 200 quarters to replace the seed and implements
consumed, and also deduct 28 quarters, or 7 per cent., upon
the whole advance of 400 quarters, then just 200 quarters
will remain to be again advanced as wages. Under these
circumstances it is self-evident that wages could not rise
above 200 quarters for 100 men, for were more than this
given to the labourers too little would remain, either for
seed and implements, or for that lowest rate of profit which
will induce the farmer to cultivate.

It is obvious that the maximum of wages may be raised,
either by the cultivation of land of a better quality, or by
improvements in the effective powers of industry; and that
it may be lowered, either by resorting to poorer soils, or by
a falling off in the effective powers of industry. In an
improving country better modes of culture are gradually
introduced, and labour is more effectually applied, particularly in manufactures. But the effect of such improvements, in raising the maximum of wages, is in general counterbalanced by the necessity of resorting to inferior soils for
the supply of food and material.

The circumstances which raise the maximum of wages to
the highest point are those in which an old and thickly-
peopled country, excelling in manufacturing industry, carries
on a perfectly free trade with new and thinly-peopled coun-

tries, in which none but soils of first-rate quality are under tillage. A simple illustration will demonstrate this.

If a master manufacturer employ 100 labourers, who fabricate for him 428 suits of clothing, and if, from the inferior quality of the soil under cultivation, he is obliged to give 200 suits for the materials he works up, it is evident that the highest point to which the wages of the 100 labourers can ascend will be 200 suits of clothing; because if more were given for labour the capitalist would have less than the lowest rate of profit, which is necessary to induce him to continue in business.

Now, let an unrestricted commerce in raw materials be established with a new country, cultivating none but first-rate soils, and let raw materials be in consequence so reduced in value, as compared with wrought goods, that the manufacturer can purchase his raw material for 100, instead of for 200 suits of clothing; and immediately the maximum of wages, for the 100 labourers, will rise from 200 to 300 suits, because the capitalist, obtaining 428 suits and advancing only 100 for materials, may give 300 to his labourers, and yet retain 28 suits, or 7 per cent. upon his whole advance of 400 suits. Measured in clothing, maximum wages will have risen 50 per cent., measured in raw produce they will appear to have risen 300 per cent.

England having acquired in manufacturing industry an efficacy unexampled in the history of the world, and having the new countries of her vast colonial empire open to her commerce on principles of perfect reciprocity, is placed in that precise situation in which the maximum of wages may be elevated to the highest attainable point. But the vast, the incalculable advantages of this situation cannot be developed without the adoption by the Government of an extended scheme of colonization.

The Minimum of Wages.

The minimum below which wages cannot permanently fall, consists in a quantity of the necessaries and conveniences of life sufficient to preserve the labourer in working condition, and to induce him to keep up the race of labourers. The point, below which wages cannot fall, is not a fixed and immutable point, but is, on the contrary, liable to considerable variation. The shelter and clothing indispensable in one country may be unnecessary in another. A labourer in Hindostan may continue to work with perfect vigour while receiving a supply of clothing which would be insufficient to preserve a labourer in Russia from perishing. Even in countries situated in the same climate, different habits of living will often occasion variations in the minimum of wages as considerable as those which are produced by natural causes.

The labourer in Ireland will rear a family under circumstances which would not only deter an English workman from marriage, but would force him on the parish for personal support. Now, it is certain that a gradual introduction of capital into Ireland, accompanied by such a diffusion of instruction amongst the people as would impart to them a taste for the comforts of life, might raise the minimum of wages in that country to an equality with their minimum in England; and we can conceive a succession of impoverishing and calamitous causes, which might so reduce the spirit of the people of England as to render them satisfied with the scanty pittance that the labourer obtains in the sister island. Alterations, however, in the minimum of wages cannot be suddenly effected. So far as this minimum depends upon climate, it is unchangeable; and even so far as it is determined by the habits of living, and the established scale of comfort, it can be effected only by those circumstances of prosperity or decay, and by those moral causes of instruction and civilization, which are ever gradual in their operation. The minimum of wages, therefore, though it varies under different climates, and with the different stages of national improvement, may, in any given time and place, be regarded as very nearly stationary.

On the Circumstances which determine the Point at which actual Wages settle.

We have seen that the *minimum* of wages is that quantity of the products of industry which climate and custom render necessary, in order to support the labourer while at work, and to induce him to keep up the race of labourers; and it has appeared that the *maximum* of wages is that quantity of the products of industry which remains after replacing the advances, not consisting of wages, and paying the capitalist the lowest rate of profit, which will induce him to continue the work of production.

Now, when climate and custom have fixed the minimum below which the reward of labour cannot fall, and when the quality of the soil, the skill with which labour is applied, and the degree of freedom which is allowed to trade, have determined the maximum beyond which it cannot rise, what is the precise circumstance which fixes the point at which actual wages settle?

In order to put this important question in a more exact and definite form, we will assume that the minimum wages of the labourer are five quarters of corn a-year, and that the minimum profit, for the sake of which the capitalist will make advances, is 7 per cent.; and we will suppose that a farmer, by employing 100 labourers, and advancing 500 quarters of corn for seed and implements, obtains a reproduction of 1605 quarters. In this case, what is to determine the wages which the 100 labourers shall receive? They may receive only 500 quarters, should wages fall to the minimum, or they may receive 1000 quarters, should wages rise to the maximum; because, as the farmer obtains a reproduction of 1605 quarters, he may, in addition to his advance of 500 quarters for seed and implements, pay 1000 quarters to his 100 labourers, and still have, upon this whole advance of 1500 quarters, the minimum profit of 7 per cent., which is sufficient to induce him to continue his business. What then determines whether the 100 labourers shall receive as their wages 500 quarters or 1000 quarters, or some medium quantity between these two extremes?

The answer to this question is, that the one and the only cause which can determine where, between the maximum and minimum, the wages of these 100 labourers shall be fixed, is the proportion between the number of labourers and the quantity of that component part of our farmer's capital which he can exchange for labour. A mere statement of the relation between the amount of the capital and the quantity of the labour will render this self-evident.

How the Proportion between Capital and Labour regulates actual Wages.

The farmer, on commencing business, commands, we will say, a capital of 1000 quarters of corn; 500 quarters of which he advances for seed and implements. Over and above his necessary expenditure for these component parts of agricultural capital, he has but 500 quarters disposable; and therefore it is physically impossible that he should give to his 100 labourers more than those 500 quarters as their wages.

The farmer obtains a reproduction of 1605 quarters; but if 605 quarters of these are absorbed in the current expenses of his family, his capital, at the commencement of the second year, will remain exactly the same as it was at the commencement of the first, and any increase of wages will continue to be impossible.

But supposing that our farmer, out of the 605 quarters formerly devoted to the current expenses of his family, contrives to save 250 quarters, and adds them to his capital of 1000 quarters, then it will immediately become possible for an advance of wages to take place; and assuming that the number of labourers remain as before, an advance of wages equal to the increase of capital necessarily will take place; the 100 labourers receiving 725 quarters instead of 500 quarters. For when the farmer, in order to extend his cultivation, makes an addition to his capital, he will require a greater number of hands, and will seek to tempt them into his employ by the offer of higher wages. But as the increase of capital is supposed to be general, all other capitalists will require additional hands as well as our farmer, and will be offering higher wages also. All the capitalists will be unwilling to let their additional capital lie idle for want of hands, and, with the twofold object of retaining their own labourers, and of obtaining those of their neighbours, will go on advancing wages, until the whole of their additional capital is absorbed.

Assuming that all the labourers are already employed, and that no addition is made to their numbers, it is morally certain that the whole of every new accumulation of capital will assume the form of increased wages, until the reward of the labourer has reached its maximum. New accumulations of capital are made for the sake of obtaining advantage therefrom. But it is impossible that new accumulations of capital should be advantageously employed, unless labourers can be procured. The new capital, accumulated for the purpose of gaining an advantage by the employment of labourers, comes into the market and bids for hands; the old capital, in order to retain its hands, is compelled to bid against the new, and this process goes on until the whole existing capital is invested in wages, seed, materials, and machinery. But as a given number of hands can use only a given quantity of seed, materials, and machinery, these ingredients or component parts of capital cannot be increased, while the quantity of labour remains the same; and therefore it is only in the form of increased wages that the new accumulations of capital can appear.

When the number of labourers remains the same, nothing can prevent new accumulations of capital from appearing under the form of increased wages, except such an intimate understanding and concert amongst capitalists, as would induce each individual of the class, instead of seeking for additional hands, to allow all his new accumulations of capital to remain idle and unproductive. But the supposition of an intimate concert amongst capitalists, for such a purpose, involves this manifest contradiction and absurdity—namely, that they accumulate capital for the sake of employing it advantageously, at the same time that they resolve not to employ it at all. If there were an understanding that all new capital should be kept unemployed, no new accumulation would take place. Whenever new accumulations do take place, they supply a complete demonstration that no combination for the purpose of not employing them exists. If such new accumulations are made, it is in order that they may be employed; and if they are employed the quantity of labour, and the state of knowledge in applying mechanical power remaining the same, there is no form in which they can appear, except in that of increased wages.

On this principle, if our farmer, employing, as before, 100 labourers, advancing 500 quarters of corn as seed and implements, and obtaining a reproduction of 1605 quarters, were, out of the 605 quarters formerly devoted to the current expenses of his family, to save 500 quarters instead of 250 quarters, then the second 250 quarters thereby added to his capital would, like the first, take the form of increased wages, and the reward of the 100 labourers, which had before risen from 500 to 750 quarters, would now rise to 1000 quarters. Here wages would have reached their maximum;

for the farmer, advancing 500 quarters for seed, and 1000 quarters for labour, and obtaining a reproduction of 1605 quarters, would gain no more than the minimum profit of 7 per cent., which, by the supposition, is necessary, to induce him to carry on his business.

Under these circumstances, it is plain that if the number of labourers did not increase, wages would continue at their maximum. Should the labouring class, during the increase of capital and advance of wages, have acquired a taste for superior modes of living, the minimum, below which wages cannot fall without reducing the supply of labour, might be made to coincide with the maximum, beyond which they cannot rise without suspending the employment of capital. When the coincidence of minimum and maximum wages is brought about by superior habits of living among the people, raising the former to the level of the latter, the labouring classes will be in the most affluent condition in which, in the nature of things, it is possible they should be placed.

This affluent condition can be preserved to the labouring classes so long only as they may refuse to burthen themselves with families sufficient to keep up the race, unless they receive the highest wages which can be paid, without trenching upon the minimum rate of profit. An increase in the number of labourers, without a contemporaneous and proportional increase in the quantity of those ingredients of capital by which labour is maintained, is inevitably followed by a decline of wages. While our farmer's capital consists of seed and implements sufficient to employ 100 labourers, and of a quantity of necessaries sufficient to pay them wages at the rate of ten quarters of corn per man, it is physically impossible that he should, with this capital, give employment to 110 labourers, at the same wages.

It necessarily follows, from the principles of rent, that when, on the last land resorted to, the smallness of the produce obtained deprives the farmer of the power of giving his labourers more than is sufficient for the support of animal life, the high rent which competition causes to be paid for all the more fertile soils, reduces the cultivator of the best to the same level with the cultivator of the worst, and brings down, universally, the maximum of wages to the minimum.

Hitherto we have taken our proofs and illustrations from agricultural labour, because in agriculture the principal things expended, such as food and seed, being homogeneous, with the things reproduced, we are enabled to form a direct comparison between the quantities expended and the quantities reproduced, and thus to give a simplicity and distinctness to our illustrations which could not otherwise be obtained. The principles, however, which regulate wages in agriculture also regulate them in manufactures. Where, as is now the case in this country, competition is allowed to operate, the value of the common labour employed in producing the first necessaries of life will regulate the value of all other kinds of labour, allowance being made for different degrees of hardship and of hazard, and for the time and expense required in learning a trade.

Beyond a certain Point, the Proportion between Capital and Labour ceases to have any influence on Wages.

It has appeared that minimum wages are fixed by climate and by the habits of living prevalent among the labouring classes; that maximum wages are determined by the quality of the soil under cultivation, and by the skill with which labour is applied; and that the point at which actual wages settle is regulated by the proportion which exists between the number of labourers to be maintained and the quantity of those ingredients of capital which are destined for their maintenance.

The ratio between labour and capital appears sometimes to be considered as the only regulator of wages. If the condition of the great body of the people be easy and comfortable, it is contended that all that is necessary to keep it so is to make capital increase as fast as population; or, on the other hand, to prevent population from increasing faster than capital; and that, if the condition of the people be not easy and comfortable, it can be made so only by quickening the rate at which capital increases, or by retarding the rate at which population increases.

This is taking a narrow and incomplete view of the circumstances which regulate wages. The ratio between labour and capital is not the only cause; it is but one out of the several causes by which wages are governed. When climate and custom have determined the point below which the reward of labour cannot fall, and when the quality of the soil, and the skill with which industry is applied, have fixed the maximum beyond which it cannot rise, then the ratio between population and capital, or, more correctly, between the quantity of labour and the quantity of the ingredients of capital destined for its maintenance, determines the intermediate point at which actual wages settle. But, though labour and capital should go on increasing in the same proportion, and though they should constantly preserve the same ratio to each other, yet the necessity of resorting to inferior soils might gradually reduce the maximum of wages until it coincided with the extreme minimum, below which labour cannot be sustained. At this point the supply of labour could be no further increased; and if habits of frugality amongst the opulent classes continued to convert revenue into capital, the ratio of capital to population might go on increasing, without producing the slightest advance of wages.

When, in the progress of wealth and population, wages and profits have fallen to their minimum, and when the next quality of land to be taken in cannot be made to yield a reproduction sufficient to pay these minimum wages and to replace advances with minimum profits, then that which is saved from revenue to be added to capital cannot be employed at home, and, unless poured out upon the fertile wastes of colonial dependencies, will be invested in foreign loans and foreign adventures. At this point the most rapid accumulation of capital, though going on while population remained stationary, could have no possible influence on wages.

On the Effect of Machinery upon Wages.

From the principles established in the preceding sections, it must be evident that, in whatever degree the employment of machinery may diminish the cost of production, it must in the same degree raise maximum or possible wages. Assuming, as before, that 7 per cent. is the lowest rate of profit for the sake of which industry will be continued, then if a farmer employing 100 labourers, with an expenditure of 500 quarters for seed and implements, could raise 749 quarters, the maximum wages of the 100 men, should no rent be paid, would be 200 quarters, or two quarters per man. Now, suppose that the farmer, by introducing a threshing machine, a winnowing machine, and a sowing machine, can raise 749 quarters from the land under cultivation, with the labour of 50 instead of 100 men, then it is self-evident that maximum or possible wages will be doubled, and will rise from two quarters to four quarters per man. Before the introduction of these machines, it was physically impossible that any effort of prudence, any diminution of the supply of labour, or any increase in the demand for it, could enable the labourers to earn, as their permanent wages, more than two quarters per man; but, now that the cost of production has been lowered by the employment of machinery, an increase in the demand for labour, or a diminution in its supply, may double wages. A capability of bettering the condition of the working people has been created —the obstacle (formerly insuperable) to their improvement has been removed.

But the practically important questions are—Would improvement really take place when it ceased to be impossible? Would *actual* wages rise because *maximum* wages had risen? Let us see.

The employment of the machines has caused an enormous

increase in the profits of the farmer. While his produce, equivalent to 749 quarters, remains as before, his expenditure, which was 500 quarters for seed and implements, and 200 quarters for wages for 100 men, is now reduced to 500 quarters for seed and implements, with 100 quarters for wages for fifty men. His profit is therefore raised from 7 to 24 per cent. Now this increased rate of profit, occasioned by the diminished cost of production, will be followed by an increase in actual as well as in maximum wages.

The 100 quarters which the farmer formerly paid as wages to fifty men, and which are now added to his profits, he cannot eat, and he will not destroy. He will expend them, either unproductively as revenue, or productively as capital. Should he expend them unproductively, upon an additional quantity of articles of dress and furniture produced within the country, they will go to pay the wages of the additional number of labourers required to fabricate this additional supply of home-made goods. Should he expend them unproductively upon foreign luxuries, they will go to pay the wages of the additional number of labourers, required to produce the additional quantity of home-made goods, with which the additional supply of foreign luxuries must be purchased. In either case the unproductive expenditure of the 100 quarters, added to the farmer's profits, will create a new demand for labour, exactly equal to the quantity of labour thrown out of employ by the introduction of the machines. The diminished demand for agricultural labour will be balanced by the increased demand for manufacturing labour, and the aggregate demand will remain undiminished. The change of occupation will, in the first instance, be accompanied by considerable local distress; but after the new proportions between the agricultural and manufacturing populations have been adjusted, the same number of labourers will be employed at the same rate of wages as before. On the supposition, therefore, that the farmer expends the whole of his increased profits unproductively, the ultimate effect will be, that maximum wages will be increased, while actual wages will remain unchanged. The quantities of raw materials and food, the funds for employing and maintaining labour, will remain as before; and should no variation take place in the numbers to be employed and maintained, wages will remain as before.

But when the introduction of the machines increased the farmer's profit from 7 to 24 per cent., the whole of this increased profit would not be expended unproductively. Increasing profits always occasion a more rapid accumulation of capital, and an increase of productive expenditure. We have therefore to consider what effect would be produced upon actual wages by the more rapid accumulation of capital, and the increased productive expenditure consequent upon the employment of the machines.

Previous to the employment of the machines, the farmer obtained, from the most inferior soils then under tillage, the rate of profit requisite to induce him to invest capital in cultivation. He can now obtain this rate of profit from lands which could not before be tilled. When the expenditure, upon a given quantity of land, was 700 quarters, the lowest quality of soil which could be cultivated with the minimum profit of 7 per cent. must have yielded 749 quarters; now that the machines have reduced the expenditure upon this quantity of land to 600, a quality of soil yielding 642 will afford this rate of profit; a new and extensive field for the employment of accumulating capital will be created; that portion of the farmer's increased profits which he adds to his capital will be employed in bringing additional land into tillage, an increased quantity of subsistence will be raised, and, unless the supply of labour should increase in the same proportion, actual wages will advance.

The employment of improved machinery in manufactures

would produce precisely similar effects. Let us take the instance of the power-loom, and, for the sake of distinctness, let us trace the result in figures.

A manufacturer's expenditure is, in the first instance, raw material and wear and tear, equivalent to 500 quarters, and wages to 100 hand-loom weavers, equivalent to 200 quarters, and with this expenditure he fabricates cloth equivalent to 749 quarters. He subsequently introduces the power-loom, which, by enabling him to get the same work done by fifty labourers, effects a saving of the wages formerly advanced to the other fifty, who are thrown out of employ. The things constituting the wages thus saved, the manufacturer will not destroy—he will advance them either in purchasing or in producing other things; and in either case the aggregate quantity of food and clothing appropriated to the maintenance of the labouring classes will suffer no diminution. The new distribution of employment will, for a considerable period, be accompanied by great privation and distress; but when a sufficient number of the hand-loom weavers, for whose work there is a diminished demand, shall be transferred to those other trades, in which there is an increased demand, there will not be, upon the whole, any reduction in actual wages, even upon the supposition that the whole saving in the cost of production is expended unproductively, and that no addition is made to those ingredients of capital which are applicable to the maintenance of labour. But this supposition would be contrary to fact. The saving which the introduction of improved machinery would effect in the cost of producing manufactured necessaries, would speedily occasion an increased creation of the funds applicable to the maintenance of labour; and unless a proportional increase should at the same time take place in the supply of labour, would cause actual wages to advance. The demand for labour would be rendered either more intense or more extensive, or, in other words, either the same number of labourers would be employed at higher wages, or else a greater number at the same wages. The reduction in the cost of preparing wrought goods, occasioned by the employment of machinery in manufactures, reduces the value of that portion of the farmer's advances which consists of clothing, furniture, and implements, and thereby enables him to obtain additional supplies of food and raw materials from tracts which could not formerly be tilled. Let us take an example.

We will assume that, before the introduction of improved machinery in manufactures, that part of the farmer's advances which consists of wrought goods is of equal value with that part which consists of raw produce. In this case, if he advance 100 quarters as food and seed, he must also advance clothing, furniture, and implements equivalent to 100 quarters; and he will be unable to cultivate, with the minimum profit of 7 per cent., any land which does not yield to this advance a produce of 214 quarters. Now let the employment of improved machinery in manufactures diminish by one-half the productive cost, and the value of wrought goods, and the farmer's advance, which was before equivalent to 200 quarters, will now be equivalent only to 150 quarters; and he will be able to cultivate, with the minimum of 7 per cent., land yielding only 160½ quarters. Tracts which could not formerly be reclaimed from their original wild and forest state, will now be brought under the plough, and there will not only be a greatly increased demand for agricultural labour, but large additional supplies of food and raw material will be raised, to maintain and employ a more numerous manufacturing population.

Machines work, but do not eat. When they displace labour, and render it disposable, they at the same time displace and render disposable the real wages, the food and clothing, which maintained it. The aggregate fund for the support of labour is not diminished, and, therefore, unless the numbers to be maintained should increase, each individual, as soon as the free subsistence and free labour are re-adjusted to each other, will have the same command of the necessaries of life as before. But machines not only leave the aggregate fund for the maintenance of labour undiminished, they actually increase it. They are employed, because they reduce productive cost; and whether such reduction take place in agriculture or in manufactures, it allows cultivation to extend over districts which could otherwise be tilled, and causes additional funds for the maintenance of labour to be created. When a machine is employed in agriculture, the quantity of food and clothing expended in raising a given produce is reduced; and when it is employed in manufactures, the value of the clothing and implements expended in raising a given produce is reduced; and, therefore, in either case the plough is driven over regions into which cultivation could not otherwise extend—the same effect is produced as if increased natural fertility had descended on the soil—the fund for the maintenance of labour is enlarged, and the same numbers will obtain higher wages, or additional numbers will obtain employment.

Mr. Ricardo has stated an hypothetical case, in which the employment of machinery might diminish the fund for the maintenance of labour, and injure the working classes. The case is this. Should any number of labourers, now employed in producing the necessaries of life, be withdrawn from that occupation, and employed in constructing machines, the immediate consequence would be a diminution in the quantity of the necessaries of life; and as the diminished quantity would have to be divided amongst the same number of persons as before, a less quantity would fall to the share of each individual, and real wages would be reduced. The diminution of the funds for the maintenance of labour, and the consequent fall of real wages, could only be temporary. As soon as the machines were completed, the labourers employed in constructing them would again become disposable for the production of necessaries, while the increased efficiency of industry, occasioned by a more extended application of mechanical power in aid of labour, would lead to extended tillage, and cause augmented supplies of food and raw material to be raised from soils which could not before remunerate the cultivator.

It is to be observed that this hypothetical case, put by Mr. Ricardo, never occurs in practice. The labourers employed in agriculture, and in manufacturing necessary articles of clothing and furniture, are never withdrawn from these occupotions for the purpose of constructing machines.* If, in any given year, the manufacture of machinery were to increase ten-fold, such increase would not occasion, even in that same year, any perceptible diminution in the supply of the necessaries of life.

The only case in which the employment of machinery can in practice diminish the funds for the maintenance of labour, is that in which the machinery is worked, not by mechanical, but by animal power. Should 100 labourers, employed in spade husbandry, consume 200 quarters of corn, and produce 220 quarters, the farmer, who advanced their consumption, would obtain 20 quarters as his profit. Now, let the plough be substituted for the spade, and horses for labourers, and then it is possible that the profits of the farmer may be increased, while the funds for the maintenance of labour are diminished. For if 20 horses, consuming 40 quarters, can do the work of 50 men, consuming 100 quarters, the farmer's whole expenditure will be reduced from 200 quarters to 140 quarters, and his return of 220 quarters to this reduced expenditure will leave 80 quarters instead of 20 quarters as his profit. But in this ·case the fund for the maintenance of labour would be reduced to the whole extent of the consumption of the horses. There will be 50 agricultural labourers thrown out of employment; but there will not be, as if the ploughs were worked by

* See Senior's able Lectures on Wages.

a non-food-consuming power, an equivalent supply of subsistence set free to support them in other occupations.

It is to be remarked, however, that the injurious effect of substituting horse-power for human labour would be gradually counteracted by the extended tillage, rendered practicable by the diminution effected in the cost of production. While the farmer employed in spade husbandry 100 men, consuming 200 quarters, he could not cultivate, with the minimum profit of seven per cent., any land yielding to this expenditure a less produce than 214 quarters. But when the substitution of ploughs and horses reduces his expenditure from 200 to 140 quarters, he can immediately extend cultivation over inferior soils, yielding to this reduced expenditure a produce of only 150 quarters ; and thus, by the extension of tillage, the funds for the maintenance of labour would be again enlarged. In a country not exporting the raw produce of the soil, the permanent interest of the working classes must always be promoted by the substitution of a cheaper for a more expensive instrument of production. When cheaper instruments of production are employed, maximum or possible wages are raised, and unless the supply of labour increases with the increased power of extending cultivation over inferior soils, actual wages are made to approximate to their maximum.

The funds for the maintenance of labour receive their greatest possible increase when, in the working of machines, horse-power is superseded. In this case human subsistence is augmented, not only by the extension of tillage rendered practicable by the reduction in the cost of production, but also by the whole quantity of produce which the horses formerly consumed. This most important augmentation in the supply of human subsistence has now commenced. Already in this country steam is superseding horses ; and it is scarcely possible to measure the extent to which this supplanting process may be carried. In a few years draught horses may disappear from all the great lines of traffic throughout England; and it seems not improbable that, at no distant period, the plough and the harrow will be moved by steam, as well as the carriage and the waggon. Upon the funds for the maintenance of labour, the substitution of steam for cattle will have the same effect as that which would be produced by doubling the fertility of the soil. There will be an unprecedented increase in the demand for labour; double the number of people may be employed at the same wages, or the same number at double wages.

From this examination of the results of machinery, it appears that all inventions for abridging labour and diminishing the cost of production, with the exception of those in which cattle are employed as the moving power, augment the funds for the maintenance of labour, and have the effect of increasing both maximum and actual wages. It also appears that the general good which results from the employment of new and improved machinery is accompanied by partial evil. While the public acquires additional wealth, the individuals who are supplanted in their accustomed occupations are reduced to poverty. Humanity and justice demand that those who thus suffer for the public good should be relieved at the public expense. Whenever a new application of mechanical power throws a particular class of operatives out of employment, a national fund should be provided to aid them in betaking themselves to other occupations. It is a disgrace to the Legislature and to the country that the numerous body of hand-loom weavers should have been left so long in misery and destitution, and toiling to the death in hopeless competition with the power-loom. A comprehensive plan for their relief ought to have been one of the earliest measures of the reformed Parliament.

*On the Manner in which the relative efficacy of British
and of Foreign Labour limits the Amount of Money-
wages in this Country.*

It may be assumed, as a proposition not open to controversy, that in countries exporting the same description of
manufactured goods, the money-wages of the operatives employed in the preparation of such goods, other things remaining the same, will gravitate towards a common level. Should
England and Germany export cottons and woollens to America,
and should the advantages, with regard to the production of
these articles be equal in the two countries, then it would be
evidently impossible for the English manufacturer to pay
higher money-wages than the German. But, on the other
hand, should England possess an advantage over Germany
with regard to the cheapness of.fuel, to the efficiency of machinery, or to the skill and energy with which manual labour
is applied; then, in either of these cases, the English manufacturer who prepared cottons and woollens for the foreign
market, could afford to pay higher money-wages than the
German to the extent of the superiority possessed. For example, should the superiority possessed by England be such as
to enable 100 operatives to execute in this country the same
quantity of work which it required 125 to execute in Germany,
then the English capitalist could afford to advance, as the
wages of 100, the same sum which might be advanced in
Germany as the wages of 125. Under the circumstances
assumed, money-wages would remain 25 per cent. higher in
England than in Germany.

For a long series of years England possessed such superior
advantages in manufacturing industry, that she was enabled to
execute, with a given number of hands, a much greater quantity of work than that which could be executed by the same
number of hands in other countries; and the necessary consequence was, that money-wages became considerably higher

in England than on the continent of Europe. While the wars
of the French revolution paralysed the industry of the continent, England, mistress of the seas, enjoying internal security,
and employed in developing the new mechanical power created
by her Watts and Arkwrights, was possessed of exclusive
advantages, which conferred upon the produce of any given
quantity of her labour a value far exceeding that which, under
the then existing circumstances, it was possible for the produce
of the same quantity of continental labour to acquire. It
would be scarcely too much to say that, in some branches of
manufacture, one English operative, during the early development and application of the new mechanical power, could
execute a greater quantity of work than that which could be
performed by 100 operatives in other manufacturing countries.
On the lowest average estimate, the goods produced by one
pair of hands in England were of greater value than the goods
produced by ten pair of hands out of England. The English
manufacturer, who sent his fabrics to the countries of the mines,
received, in proportion to the labour employed upon them, a
much larger quantity of the precious metals than that which
could be obtained by the foreign manufacturer. As the
produce of a given quantity of English labour exchanged for a
greater quantity of gold than the produce of the same quantity of foreign labour, the English labourer was enabled to
command higher money-wages than the foreign. High money-
wages created a high money demand for provisions, and for
all home productions, the cost of which the new mechanical
power had not reduced. The value of all foreign productions,
including the precious metals, fell in relation to the produce
of domestic labour, to that labour itself, to land, to taxation,
and to the public debt. The condition of the industrious
classes improved through the combined operation of these
causes. While money wages and profits, estimated in money,
rose, the prices of those articles of comfort and convenience to
which the progressive improvements in mechanical power

could be applied, gradually declined; the prices of foreign commodities, whether necessaries or comforts, did not rise in an equal proportion to the rise in money-wages, while the high value of the produce of given quantities of labour in relation to land, and to other descriptions of fixed property, tended to abate the pressure of taxation. Under these circumstances, the real reward of labour, and the general scale of comfort, became higher in England than on the continent of Europe. The world became tributary to England. The extent of the superiority which the people of this country acquired from the exclusive possession of the improvements in mechanical power, and from the monopoly of commerce, growing out of the incidents of the revolutionary war, it would be difficult to estimate. It appears to be generally admitted, that it was the almost miraculous increase in the productive power of British industry, coincident with the war, which supplied the means by which the war was carried on. While some have affirmed that " James Watt was the real conqueror of Napoleon," others have seen in the inexhaustible resources so suddenly and so opportunely conferred upon England, a special interposition of Providence for the deliverance of Europe. " The war was unquestionably one of finance. It could not have been carried on in Europe without an enormous and wholly unexampled expenditure. It was necessary to pay the thrones of the whole continent even to fight for themselves. Without our loans, they must have submitted and increased the vassals and the armies of France. The power of lending is not unlimited; and England had long felt that she had reached the natural limit of taxation. To avoid this pressure by sharing it with America, she had even hazarded and suffered the loss of her colonies. And just then, as the very crisis was approaching which was to lay upon her a burthen which she had never calculated on bearing, or being able to bear—a crisis, too, which, near as it was, no man had been able to foresee, an extraordinary means of wealth was put into her hands; sustained and followed by the sudden discovery of the most powerful instrument of skill and labour ever given to man; and the combined effort *did* enable England to subsidize all Europe, to fight the universal tyrant in defence of the universal cause, to pour out millions upon millions amidst universal bankruptcy, and, finally, to achieve a miraculous deliverance. What can be more complete than the proof, except the actual pouring down of a stream of gold from heaven before our eyes? The stream of gold was actually poured; and though it did not come in the shape of miracle, yet its source might not be the less providential for its winding its way through the ten thousand channels of society to issue in the noblest use of the wealth of nations. Extensive interests were dependent on success; the ultimate overthrow of the revolution with all its evils, the restoration of European order, and the palpable triumph of sound principles in government and religion, were so clearly connected with this country, that we, at least, should not be surprised to find that its success had been provided for by the great Protector of human happiness." *

In achieving the deliverance of Europe, England resigned some portion of the exclusive advantages by which the means of continuing the contest had been supplied. With the restoration of peace, the industry of the Continent revived; the seas were opened to the flags of the world; and the facility of international communication extended to other commercial countries that knowledge in the application of scientific power which had for so long a period been confined to England. The difference between the efficacy of British and of foreign labour became less and less. The goods produced in England, by a single pair of hands, would no longer exchange for the goods produced in other countries by many pairs of hands; and as the produce of British industry ex-

* "Blackwood's Magazine," for October, 1842.

changed for a less quantity of foreign productions, including the precious metals, money-wages, and the prices of home productions, necessarily declined. It is now too late to inquire to what extent the depression occasioned by the transition from war to peace might have been mitigated by the early adoption of an enlightened course of commercial policy. Erroneous legislation aggravated the evil. The restrictive system, of which we set the example, has been turned against us. The industrial processes indigenous to England have been acclimated in other countries. Our former customers are our present rivals. How this state of things might have been prevented, postponed, or mitigated, is not the problem which has now to be solved; the duty which devolves upon the statesman of the present day is, to save the industrious millions from the effects of a transition partly resulting from the progress of knowledge, and of improvement in other countries, and partly created by the tariff war, waged universally against British commerce.

We must ascertain the character of the disease before we can apply an appropriate remedy; we must probe the wound to the bottom before we can determine the extent of the operation which it may be necessary to perform. Before proceeding to the consideration of practical measures, it will be expedient to revert to the circumstances which have occasioned the progressive decline of wages in England, and to measure the extent to which, if not counteracted, the depression is likely to proceed.

The superior advantages which have hitherto rendered the produce of a given quantity of English labour more valuable than the produce of the same quantity of foreign labour, and which have consequently enabled the English to command higher wages than the continental operative, are, mechanical inventions, manual dexterity, and productive coal mines. Now, ever since the termination of the wars of the French revolution, foreign countries have been approaching nearer and nearer to an equality with England, with regard to these advantages ; and the consequence has been, that the value of the products of foreign industry has been gradually rising, in relation to the products of British industry ; or, to express the same result in other words, the value of the produce of British industry has been gradually falling, in relation to the products of foreign industry, including in these products the precious metals. This decline in the value of British goods involved, as its inevitable consequence, a decline in money-wages. As the master manufacturer obtained a less quantity of gold for the produce of the same quantity of labour, his only alternative was, to pay less wages, or to carry on a losing trade, terminating in bankruptcy, and in a total cessation of wages.

Should the causes now adverted to continue in operation, wages must continue to decline. Should foreign countries attain to an equality with England, as regards the advantages which give efficacy to industry, English wages must fall to the foreign level. And should our Continental rivals, in their rapid progress of improvement, acquire superiority in manufacturing any principal staple for exportation, then wages in England will continue to decline, not only until they shall have touched the Continental level, but until they shall have sunk below it. Let the comparative efficacy of industry be such that it requires in England 110 pair of hands to produce, for exportation, the same goods which can be supplied by 100 pair of hands in rival countries, and then the money-wages of the English operative will fall 10 per cent. below the foreign level. The circumstances which may be expected to affect the comparative efficacy of British and of foreign industry form one of the most important subjects of inquiry which, in the actual condition of England, can be brought under the consideration of the practical statesman.

The main causes which have hitherto conferred upon the

produce of a given quantity of British labour, the power of purchasing the produce of a greater quantity of foreign labour, are, as has been already stated, the employment of superior machinery, greater energy and skill in the application of manual labour, and the possession of more accessible coal mines. Is it reasonable to suppose that, in the present circumstances of the world, England can maintain a permanent monopoly of the advantages which enable a given number of hands to execute a greater quantity of work in one locality than another? In the actual state of knowledge and of international communication, the adoption of the latest improvements in scientific power cannot be confined to any particular country. A rigid enforcement of laws against the exportation of machinery might possibly retard, but could not ultimately prevent the inevitable result. If the exportation of our machines could be prevented, the makers of our machines would be induced to emigrate; and in the long run, we should lose the advantage of manufacturing superior machines for the foreign market, without being able to secure their exclusive application. As regards energy and skill in the application of manual labour, it would be presumptuous to assume that the English operative will continue ever superior to the robust and persevering German. These artificial advantages rival nations will acquire.

In the employment of machinery, and in the efficacy of manual labour, England cannot continue to retain any marked superiority over other manufacturing countries. With respect, however, to the natural advantage of accessible coal fields, the case may be different. Coal abounds in Belgium, and in Prussia; but it is believed that the coal of these countries is of an inferior quality to that found in many parts of Britain; while it is less conveniently situated, with respect to the seats of manufacturing industry. Should this be the case, then, to whatever extent the possession of the natural advantage of cheaper fuel may enable a given number of hands in England to execute a greater quantity of work than the same number of hands can execute upon the Continent, to that extent, and to that extent alone, can the English operative, who works for the foreign market, continue to receive higher money-wages than the Continental operative, who works for the same market. Other things being the same, the amount which the master manufacturer saves by the purchase of cheaper fuel, he may employ in the payment of higher wages. If, in the production of a given quantity of goods in England, ninety-five men are employed in the factory, and five in providing fuel, while in the production of the same quantity of goods upon the Continent, ninety-five men are employed in the factory, and ten in providing fuel, then the amount of money-wages which is paid to 105 workmen on the Continent, may be paid to 100 in England. But it is obvious that, under the circumstances assumed, money-wages in England could not exceed money-wages on the Continent, by more than 5 per cent. For should the English operatives succeed for a time in compelling their employers to pay money-wages exceeding the Continental level by more than the difference in the price of fuel, the inevitable consequences would be, that the English manufacturer would be undersold in the foreign market, and that the operative would be thrown out of work. No combination amongst labourers, no liberality on the part of capitalists, and no interference on the part of the Legislature, could by possibility avert these results. In a country extensively engaged in manufacturing for foreign markets, no artificial mounds can be created for damming up money-wages above the level determined by foreign competition.

*On the Manner in which the Import Duties imposed by
Foreign States on British Goods lower the Value of
British Labour.*

The effect of hostile tariffs upon wages remains to be
traced. We have seen that when the labour and capital
employed in supplying foreign markets with British fabrics
increase in a higher ratio than the labour and capital employed in foreign countries in supplying equivalents, the
money-wages of the British operative must be pressed down
below the amount which would otherwise be due to his
energy and skill. Now we shall find, upon a due consideration of the subject, that the fall of wages, occasioned
by the disproportionate increase in the labour and capital
employed in manufacturing for foreign markets, must receive
a grievous aggravation from the heavy import duties imposed
by foreign countries upon British goods.

Goods of the same kind and quality cannot be sold in the
same market at different prices. Were the efficacy of
industry greater by 10 per cent. in England than in Belgium,
and were a perfectly free trade established between the two
countries, then a bale of goods produced in England by the
labour of 100, would sell in the Belgian market for the same
sum which a similar bale produced in Belgium by the labour
of 110 would sell for; and, consequently, the money-wages
of the English might exceed by 10 per cent. the money
wages of the Belgian operatives. But the commerce between
England and Belgium, instead of being perfectly free, is
restricted by import duties. Belgium, in order to protect
her domestic manufactures, imposes a duty of 10 per cent.
ad valorem upon the importation of woollen cloths; and,
consequently, the British manufacturer who sends woollens
to the Belgian market can obtain, after the deduction of the
duty, only 90*l.* for the same quantity and quality of goods
for which the Belgian manufacturer obtains 100*l.* The

amount of the Belgian duty is deducted from English wages. If, as we have just assumed, the superior efficacy of British industry were such that 90 English operatives could execute as much work as 100 Belgians, then English wages, instead of maintaining a due proportion to the efficacy of English labour, would fall to the Belgian level.

Again, the Belgian tariff imposes a duty of 21 per cent. *ad valorem* upon certain descriptions of linen fabrics. The British manufacturer who should send such fabrics to the Belgian market, could obtain, after the deduction of the duty, only 79*l.* for a bale of the same description of linen goods for which the Belgian manufacturer obtained 100*l.*; and, consequently, if the whole of the labour, direct and indirect, employed in preparing the bale of linens were 90 in England and 100 in Belgium, the sum received as wages by 90 English labourers would be less by 21*l.* (the amount of the duty) than the sum received by 100 Belgians. In other words, the English operative employed in the linen trade could earn, notwithstanding the superior efficacy of his labour, amounting by the supposition to upwards of 10 per cent., only 17*s.* 6½*d.*, where his Belgian rival would earn 1*l.*

Previous to the recent modification of the tariff of the German Customs Union, the duties payable upon British goods, throughout the immense territory comprised within the Zolverein, were equivalent to 90 per cent. *ad valorem* upon coarse fabrics, 32 per cent. upon superior shirting, 15 per cent. upon printed cottons, worth 1*s.* 6*d.* per yard, and about 9 per cent. upon fine printed cottons, worth 2*s.* 6*d.* per yard. By the new tariff, the duty upon cotton warps is advanced from the former amount of two dollars per hundred weight to three dollars, being an increase of 50 per cent.; on worsted, and worsted and cotton mixed goods, if printed, embroidered, or *broche*, the duty is increased from 30 to 50 dollars per hundred weight, or 66 per cent.; while upon hardware the increase of duty amounts to cent per cent.

The operation of these duties, as regards comparative wages, will be immediately apparent. It is obvious that the British manufacturer, who competes with the German manufacturer in the markets of the German union, must be compensated for the whole amount of the duty which he may be required to pay, either by the superiority of British labour as compared with German labour, or by the degradation of British wages below the German level. But Germany, with her orderly and persevering population, with her coal mines, her navigable rivers, and her projected railroads, is gradually approaching towards an equality with England in all that relates to the efficacy of industry. The causes are already in full and resistless operation, which will render it impossible for the British manufacturer to retain possession of the German market, except upon the condition of a progressive reduction of wages in England.

The tariffs of the other principal states of Europe are yet more injurious than that of the German union. The import duties imposed by France limit our exports to that country to an inconsiderable amount; the charges upon imports exacted by Russia deprive us of the power of paying in manufactured goods for the enormous amount of produce which we annually receive from her; and by the Austrian tariff duties equivalent to 60 per cent. *ad valorum* are imposed upon all' kinds of cotton manufacture, upon earthenware, hardware, and woollen goods of all kinds. It would be superfluous to repeat the details of the process by which these hostile tariffs contribute to depress the wages of labour in England. The *modus operandi* is alike in all. As commodities of the same kind and quality cannot be sold in the same market at different prices, the price which the British manufacturer, who exports goods to any foreign country, can actually realize, must be less, by the amount of the import duty which he pays, than the price realized by the manufacturers of that country for similar goods. For this diminution in his receipts the British manufacturer must be indemnified, either by the superior efficacy of the labour which he employs, or by the inferior price which he pays for it. But the progress of knowledge and of improvement is gradually bringing up the efficacy of foreign labour to an equality with that of British labour; and it follows, as an inevitable consequence, that the British manufacturer who continues to work for foreign markets will be compelled to enforce a reduction in wages equivalent to the import duties charged upon his goods.

England possesses no superiority over the United States of North America as regards the advantages, whether natural or acquired, by which the efficacy of industry is increased. Within the Union there are coal fields and water power to an almost unlimited extent; some of our latest improvements in the application of mechanical power have been borrowed from the States; our transatlantic brethren are in no way inferior to us in energy, dexterity, and skill, and they grow, while we import, the raw material of our most important manufacture. There is no cause in operation which can enable a given number of hands to execute a greater quantity of work in England than in the United States. Were it not that wages are lower in England than in America, British fabrics could not be sold in the markets of the United States. In the coarser cotton fabrics, the greater cheapness of the raw material appears sufficient to indemnify the American manufacturer for the higher wages which he pays, and to enable him to compete successfully with his British rival in distant markets. Wages pressed down something below the American level, would be the condition upon which alone the British could undersell the American manufacturer in the American market, even if America could be induced to abandon her tariff, and to admit British fabrics duty free. This we cannot hope for. Under the Compromise Act, and previous to the recent modification of the American tariff, the

D

import duties were to be limited to 20 per cent. These duties have now been enormously increased, and it is the avowed design of the Whig party in the Union to adopt the protective system to such an extent as to give the American manufacturer a monopoly in the home market. Should this policy prevail, a fall of wages in England, to the lowest level at which life can be sustained, will be the melancholy condition upon which alone an extended sale of British goods in the American Union can be effected. But a result less disastrous may perhaps be anticipated. High protecting duties in favour of the manufacturers of the northern states must prove so injurious to the cultivators of the southern states that it seems not unreasonable to hope that the continuance of such duties may be successfully resisted, and the more liberal policy of the Compromise Act re-established. Let us take the most favourable view of the subject, and endeavour to estimate the relative amount of wages in England and America, under the supposition that America will consent to abandon her existing tariff, and to revert to the policy by which her import duties were to be limited to 20 per cent.

It is evident that British and American goods of the same kind and quality, must be sold to the consumer in the American market at the same price; and it is equally evident, that if the British manufacturer has to pay a charge of 20 per cent. from which his competitor is exempt, he must be enabled, either by employing fewer hands or by paying lower wages, to effect a diminution in the cost of production equivalent to the impost. But as industry is not less effective in the United States than in England, the British manufacturer cannot employ fewer hands than the American, in bringing his commodity to market; and it follows, as a necessary consequence, that the import duty imposed by America upon British goods, must fall on British wages.

The manner in which an American import duty of 20 per

cent. would affect British wages may be thus analysed. England and the United States being on a footing of equality with regard to the efficacy of their industry, an American manufacturer, after advancing 100*l.* on account of the wear and tear of machinery, fuel, and raw material, and another 100*l.* on account of wages, produces a bale of cotton goods, which he sells for 220*l.*, or at a profit of 10 per cent.; while the British manufacturer, after advancing 100*l.* for machinery, fuel, and materials, and employing the same number of hands as the American, sends to the American market a similar bale of goods, sells them there for the same price of 220*l.*, and pays the import duty of 20 per cent. or 45*l.* upon them. In this case it is self-evident that if the British manufacturer had paid, like the American, 100*l.* for wages, he would have suffered a loss of 25*l.* upon the transaction. Though the price paid by the consumers was 220*l.*, yet the price realized by the manufacturer, after the deduction of duty, was only 175*l.*; and consequently, if his profit was to be 10 per cent. his whole outlay, in sending his bale of cottons to market, could not have exceeded 158*l.* Of this sum, he must have paid 100*l.* on account of machinery, moving power, and materials (England and the United States being by the supposition on an equality in these particulars), and, consequently, the British manufacturer could have paid only 58*l.* to the same number of operatives to whom the American manufacturer paid 100*l.*

The hypothetical case thus assumed, for the sake of illustration, will perhaps be sufficient to explain the manner and degree in which the tariff of the United States tends to force down English wages below the American level. England and the United States are so nearly upon an equality with regard to all the circumstances which contribute to give efficacy to industry, that the British manufacturer cannot procure machinery, moving power, and raw material, at less cost than the American manufacturer; and it therefore follows, that when British manufactures, similar to the protected

American manufactures, are sold in the American markets, it is upon the wages of the English operative that the American import duties must ultimately fall.

It may be asked, why is it necessary that the English capitalist should dispose of his goods upon the same advantageous terms as the American capitalist? and why should not the import duty, imposed on British fabrics, be deducted from the profit of the master, instead of from the wages of the operative.

The first answer to these questions is, that the ratio in which the value of finished goods can be made to exceed the cost of their production, is not sufficient to allow of the payment of heavy import duties out of the master's profit. The second answer is, that were it even practicable to give to manufactured goods a marketable value, exceeding their productive cost in such a proportion as to leave a margin equivalent to the duty charged upon them, that duty could not be made to fall on profits, without disturbing the equilibrium which capital throughout the commercial world has a constant tendency to maintain. Profits conform to a general level more rapidly than wages; money is transferred from one country to another with little difficulty, and at little cost; labour is so transferred with considerable difficulty, and at considerable cost. A bill of exchange wafts capital across the Atlantic; to convey the operative requires an expensive voyage, the cost of which he may be unable to defray. A slight difference in the rate of profit moves masses of capital from one locality to another; a considerable difference in the amount of wages is insufficient to occasion a corresponding transference of labour. Were the English manufacturer, who prepares goods for the American market, to pay the same wages which are paid to the American operative, manufacturing profits would be less in England than in America, by the amount of the import duty cnarged on British fabrics; and the inevitable consequence would be, that manufacturing capital would migrate from England to the United States, and that the operative would be left in utter destitution. The melancholy alternative is— reduced wages, or no wages at all. Powers of production outgrowing the field of employment, foreign competition, and hostile tariffs, have already degraded, and if remedial measures be not speedily applied, must continue still farther to degrade the condition of the industrious masses, dependent upon foreign trade for the means of subsistence.

This fearful change cannot be confined to those who are directly depending upon foreign trade. The operatives employed in preparing cottons, and woollens, and linens, and hardware, for the home market, cannot command higher wages than those who may be employed in preparing similar articles for the foreign market. Unless remedial measures commensurate to the magnitude of the evil be adopted, the price of labour throughout all the manufacturing districts of the kingdom will continue to decline. Nor will the decline be limited to manual labour. The money demand for every species of personal service will become less and less. As foreign rivalry, hostile tariffs, and powers of production outgrowing the field of employment, reduce the value of the produce of British labour in relation to the produce of foreign labour, including gold and silver, foreign countries will command a greater, and England a less proportion of the precious metals circulating throughout the commercial world. The hitherto existing distribution of the metals will be progressively altered, to the disadvantage of England; and the necessary result of such alteration will be, a general fall in the price of all non-imported commodities, or, in other words, a rise in the value of money, in relation to British labour and its products.

The fall in real wages will be greater than the fall in money-wages. As the distribution of the precious metals changes to the disadvantage of England, the fall in the price of the produce of British labour will be accompanied by a rise in the price of the produce of foreign labour. Now while England continues to import corn, and other articles of food, the price of the necessaries of life in the home market must be regulated by their price in the foreign countries from which they are imported; and hence the fall in money-wages may be expected to be followed by a comparative advance in the price of food.

The prospect which lies before us is distressing. Hitherto the standard of comfort has been higher in England than in the other countries of Europe. This higher standard may now be lowered. Should the efficacy of foreign labour rise to an equality with that of British labour, English wages must descend to the foreign level; should the disproportionate increase of the capital and labour employed in foreign trade compel us to force our fabrics into markets where they are met by hostile tariffs, the wages of the labour by which they are prepared must fall, not merely to a level with the wages of equally effective labour employed upon similar goods in the country to which we may export, but to such a depth below that level, as may be determined by the amount of the import duty imposed upon our goods. The English artisan would be compelled to exchange his wheaten loaf for the black bread of the continent; to reduce his accustomed supply of animal food, and to relinquish the tea and sugar hitherto regarded as amongst the necessaries of life. The fall would be severe. It would be a descent, not from superiority to equality, but from superiority to inferiority. The condition of the industrious classes in England, with regard to food, clothing, and lodging, would sink below that of the same classes throughout the Continent of Europe. In what spirit would the calamitous vicissitude be borne? What effects might be expected to result from this progressive deterioration of the physical condition of the working classes?

On the Effect of Combinations for reducing Wages.

In order to trace the effect of combinations for lowering wages, let us suppose, in the first instance, that the farmers in an agricultural parish, in addition to their seed and implements, have each a fund of 200 quarters of corn for the maintenance of labour, which fund is advanced to fifty labourers. In this case, the real wages (estimated in corn) of each labourer will be four quarters.

Let us now suppose, in the second instance, that all the farmers of the parish enter into a combination for reducing the wages of their workmen from four to three quarters, and that to this reduction the labourers are compelled to submit. The important question is, what would be the final effects of this combination?

It is obvious that the first effect must be a great increase in the profits of the farmers. All that the labourers lost the farmers would gain.

It is equally obvious that the farmers could retain this advantage only so long as they agreed amongst themselves to employ their increased profits, not in adding to their capital, but in augmenting their unproductive expenditure. They could not employ additional capital without bidding against each other for additional hands, and thus breaking up the combination for the reduction of wages. The existence of the combination involves the necessity of devoting the whole of the increased profits resulting from it to immediate enjoyment.

This being the case, the reduction in agricultural wages gives to each farmer an additional revenue of fifty quarters of corn to be expended by his family in the decorations of dress and furniture. In the manufacturing towns, therefore, there will be an increased demand for those articles, while there will be a diminished demand for the wrought necessaries used by the agricultural labourers whose wages are reduced. But the increase in the demand for manufactured luxuries will be greater than the diminution in the demand for manufactured necessaries, because the revenue which the agricultural labourers have lost was partly expended upon food and partly upon manufactured goods; while the whole of the revenue which the farmers have gained, and which is equivalent to the whole which the labourers have lost, is expended upon manufactured luxuries. The result must therefore be a considerable increase in the demand for manufactured goods.

The increased demand for manufactured goods will create an increased demand for labour in the manufacturing towns; and in those towns, therefore, wages will advance. But if wages rise in the towns, while they fall in the country, a portion of the rural population will seek employment in the towns. A diminution in the supply of labour in the agricultural districts, threatening to contract cultivation, will therefore compel the farmers, notwithstanding their combination, to consent to an advance of wages.

But suppose that the combination for the reduction of wages extends to the towns, and that all master manufacturers agree together to reduce the wages of their workmen in the same proportion in which the farmers have reduced the wages of agricultural labour. The effects of this more extended combination it will be important to trace.

When, in the towns, the employers of labour have reduced wages by one-fourth, a considerable reduction will take place in the quantity and quality of the food consumed by the labouring classes in the towns. Hence, while the reduction of wages, and the consequent diminution in the consumption of food in the country districts, leave the farmers a greater quantity of agricultural produce to bring to market, the town demand for their produce will decline. One-fourth of the food and raw materials of necessaries, formerly consumed by the labouring class, will be unsaleable; one-fourth of the land must be thrown out of cultivation; and one-fourth of the agricultural population must be transferred to the towns, there to fabricate the increased quantity of manufactured luxuries, for which the increase of profits creates a demand.

While this process is going on, there will be a great destruction of agricultural capital, and many farmers will be involved in distress and ruin. But we assume, for the sake of argument, that notwithstanding the distress and ruin through which the class of farmers must pass in attaining their object, they nevertheless adhere to the combination, and ultimately succeed in effecting a universal reduction of one-fourth in the rate of wages. Let us endeavour to trace the consequences which would flow from this reduction.

The first effect of the universal reduction of wages would be an enormous rise in the rate of profit. We can estimate, not indeed the exact, but the proximate extent of this rise. It will be determined by the average proportion which, before they were reduced, wages bore to the whole advances of the capitalist. Thus, if wages, before they were reduced, constituted one-half of the capitalist's advances, their reduction by a fourth would diminish his advances by an eighth; and, as his return would remain the same as before, the extent of the increase of profits will immediately appear; for if, before the reduction of wages, the farmers or other capitalists advanced 100 quarters as wages, and 100 quarters for other outgoings, and obtained a reproduction of 220 quarters, or a profit of 10 per cent., then it is evident that when wages are reduced from 100 to 75, the capitalist's reproduction of 220 to his reduced expenditure of 175 will yield him a profit of 25 per cent. It is obvious that, if on the average wages constituted more than one-half of the whole advances, the rise of profits would be greater; while, if wages constituted less than one-half the whole advances, the rise of profits would be less. The principle is, that any given fall in the general rate of wages will cause a greater or less rise in the rate of profits, according as wages, on the average, form a greater or a less proportion of the capitalist's whole advances. For the purposes of our argument, it is a sufficient approximation to the actual state of things to assume that wages form one-half of the capitalist's advances; and that, therefore, a general fall of wages, to the extent of one-fourth, will raise the rate of profit, if it had been 10 per cent. before the fall of wages, to 25 per cent.

Now, the important practical questions for our consideration are—Would it be possible to keep things in this state? Would it be practicable to perpetuate this forced depression of wages and rise of profits? A little careful inquiry will convince us that it would be quite impracticable, and that the final effect of the combination would be, not to raise profits at the expense of wages, but, on the contrary, to elevate wages at the expense of profits. Let us consider, in the first place, the circumstances which would render it impracticable to keep wages at the reduced level to which the combination of employers had forced them down, and then proceed to trace the re-action and recoil by which they would ascend, not merely to their former, but to a still higher level.

To keep wages at the low level to which, by the supposition, the combination has reduced them, it would be necessary that the following circumstances, each morally impossible, should concur :—

First.—It would be necessary that the whole of the employers of labour throughout the country should expend the whole of their profits unproductively. No addition must be made to the aggregate amount of capital which they employ. The farmer must not extend his cultivation, nor the manufacturer increase his transactions. Children must not be put out to trade, but must continue to be dependent upon the profits realized by their parents, until their parents die off and make place for them to carry on business on their own account. Should any of these events occur (and unless the principles and motives of human conduct were reversed, they would occur perpetually), the combination would be neutralized, the demand for labour would be increased, and wages would advance.

Secondly.—It would be necessary, not only that all farmers and master manufacturers, actually and directly employing labour, should abstain, as above, from increasing their capital, and extending their transactions; but also that all monied capitalists, bankers, merchants, traders, annuitants, civil and military functionaries, together with all landed proprietors throughout the country, should become parties to a combination for oppressing the labourer, and inflicting positive evil and grievous injury upon themselves. The whole of these classes must spend the whole of their incomes unproductively; or, if they make savings, must hoard them. Their accumulations, when made, they must neither employ productively themselves, nor lend out to be employed productively by others. The reduction of wages has caused the rate of profit to rise to 25 per cent., and the throwing out of one-fourth of the land which supplied the labouring classes with food and the raw materials of manufactured necessaries, by limiting the necessary extent of tillage to soils of a superior quality, must have occasioned a still further increase of profits, and have raised them to 30, perhaps to 35 per cent. The natural effect of a high rate of profit is to raise the rate of interest also. If 30, or even 25 per cent. could be made by the employment of borrowed capital, individuals destitute of capital themselves, but having the skill, industry, and integrity, which command credit, might be willing to give 15 or 20 per cent. for the use of money. But if money be lent to be employed productively the combination cannot be maintained. In order to maintain it, it is necessary that persons having money at command should hoard it in strong boxes, or bury it under ground, rather than lend it at 15 or 20 per cent. Again, the combination for the reduction of wages has thrown out of cultivation one-fourth of the land which formerly supplied the labouring population with food and the materials of wrought necessaries, and has therefore occasioned a total loss of rent upon all the lands thrown out, and a considerable fall of rents upon all the better soils still remaining under tillage. In order to maintain the combination, it is further necessary that the landed proprietors should join in the league for reducing and destroying the value of their own property. They must not lend their money, or their credit, at an interest of 15 or 20 per cent. to industrious and honest tenants, who would cultivate the lands which had been thrown out, and occasion a recovery of rents; because, should they advance their money, or their credit, for such a purpose, the funds for the maintenance of labour would be increased, wages would rise, and the effect of the combination would be destroyed.

Thirdly.—It would be necessary, in order to maintain the combination, that the influx of foreign capital should be prohibited. Though all the farmers and master manufacturers throughout the country should join in the conspiracy for the reduction of wages; and though monied capitalists, and merchants, and bankers, and annuitants, and public functionaries, and landed proprietors, should enter into a solemn league and covenant to lend neither money, nor credit, to any one desirous of engaging in the work of production, yet the combination would be inoperative and abortive if the importation of foreign capital were permitted. The rate of profit has a tendency to preserve a certain level, not only throughout the several districts of the same country, but also throughout the several countries of the commercial world. Should the depression of wages, and the throwing out of inferior land, raise the rate of profit in England, in any considerable degree above the level it had ordinarily preserved, in relation to the rates of profit in Holland and in France, the disengaged and floating capital of these countries would flow into England, and there seek productive investment. The combination would therefore be ineffectual, unless the conspirators against wages could secure the co-operation of the Legislature, and obtain an Act of Parliament prohibiting the importation of food and of raw materials, and all the ingredients of directly productive capital, which constitute the fund for the maintenance of labour.

After this enumeration of the circumstances which must concur, in order to give effect to a combination for the reduction of wages, it would be superfluous to go into any argument or illustration to show that the maintenance of such a combination would be utterly impracticable. It is only necessary to trace out the process by which, were it possible, which it clearly is not, to give such a combination a brief and partial existence, it would necessarily counterwork itself, and ultimately tend, not to depress, but to elevate wages.

We have seen that the minimum below which wages cannot permanently fall, consists of that quantity of the necessaries of life which is requisite to keep up the labouring population; and we have seen that this quantity of necessaries is not a fixed immutable quantity, but varies under different climates, and under the influence of different habits of living. It is self-evident, that should wages be at their *physical* minimum, as determined by climate, a combination depressing them below this point would cut off a portion of the population; that it would diminish the supply of labour in relation to the demand; and that its ultimate effect would be, not to depress but to elevate wages. A moment's consideration will render it apparent, that should wages be at the *moral* minimum, as determined by habits of living, a combination for depressing them, if for a time successful, would be followed by similar results.

Custom is a second nature, and things not originally necessary to healthful existence become so from habit. Though the Irish peasantry, living upon potatoes and butter-milk, are nòt subjected to greater mortality than their neighbours, yet were the labouring classes in England, brought up upon the more substantial diet of bread and cheese, and butchers' meat, reduced to the less nutritious food which use has rendered not unhealthful in Ireland, debility and disease would rapidly thin their ranks. A higher rate of mortality among the labouring classes would speedily follow the establishment of a combination for reducing wages. Where there were numerous families they would be thinned by death; the delicate and infirm would sink prematurely to the grave; and while more died, fewer would be born. The cautious and the prudent, and those who were attached to the former superior scale of comfort, would abstain from marriage, and from encumbering themselves with families; and thus, by rendering deaths more numerous and births less frequent, an effectual combination for the reduction of wages, however brief its existence, would, for a whole generation, reduce the supply of labour in relation to the demand. Nothing could now prevent the recoil of wages. An effective combination for the reduction of wages would bear within it the principle of almost immediate self-destruction; and, after a brief existence, would leave wages at a higher level than that from which they had fallen. For, the instant the combination should be broken up, increased capital accumulated at home, or imported from abroad, would be employed in cultivating the land which had been abandoned, and in supplying the renewed consumption of the necessaries of life. Thus there would be an increased demand for labour acting upon a diminished supply. The supply of labour, in relation both to land and capital, would be less than before, and, therefore, upon the principles already explained, both maximum and actual wages would be higher than before.

From all that has been said it must be apparent that an effectual combination for the reduction of wages can never by possibility exist. In the first place such a combination could not be established; and, in the second place, if it could be established it could not be maintained. If not immediately broken up by productive advances made from income, or by the importation of capital from abroad, it would speedily perish by self-destruction; and its evil influence, after having for a time afflicted the labouring classes, would recoil upon the insane conspirators, lowering, instead of raising, the rate of profit, and elevating, instead of depressing, wages.

In a Country not depending upon Foreign Markets, Combinations amongst Workmen, could they be maintained, might raise Wages to their maximum, provided the supply of Labour did not increase.

The labouring classes form the great majority of every community, and, as has been already observed, a country must be considered as happy or miserable in proportion as those classes are abundantly or scantily supplied with the necessaries and comforts of life. From this principle it necessarily follows that combinations for lowering wages, could they be effectual, must be regarded as conspiracies for increasing human misery; and that combinations for raising wages, could they be effectual, must be approved as associations for the promotion of human happiness. In the whole compass of economical science the most important practical question is this, namely, Can combinations amongst the labouring classes effect a permanent increase of wages?

It is evident that, if wages were already at their maximum, a combination which should have the immediate effect of raising wages must speedily terminate in reducing them. When wages are at their maximum, profits are at their minimum; but when profits are at their minimum, an increase of wages must check production, diminish the fund for the maintenance of labour, and leave for each labourer a less quantity of the comforts and necessaries of life.

Supposing, as in our former cases, that the lowest rate of profit, for the sake of which the capitalist will continue the

work of production, is 7 per cent., then, should the farmer,
advancing 100 quarters of corn for seed, and 100 quarters for
the wages of 25 men, cultivate a tract of land yielding
214 quarters, profits would be at their minimum, and wages
at their maximum. Under those circumstances, if the 25 labourers were to combine together and refuse to work, unless
their wages were raised from 100 to 115 quarters, it is evident
that all profit would be absorbed, that the tract of land must
be abandoned, and that the 25 labourers, instead of continuing to receive the increased wages which they demanded
from the farmer, would, at no distant period, be thrown out
of work.

Now, suppose that profits, instead of being at the minimum
of 7 per cent., were 10 per cent. In this case wages might
rise so as to reduce profits by 3 per cent. before the last
quality of land under tillage would be thrown out of cultivation. Our 25 labourers might, therefore, combine until
each received as his wages four quarters and the fraction of
a quarter, instead of four quarters. But should this immediate improvement in their condition, by diminishing deaths
or increasing births, cause their numbers to increase from
25 to 27, the ultimate result would be, not an advance, but a
decline of wages. When the farmer, cultivating a tract of
land yielding 220 quarters, advanced 100 quarters as seed
and 100 quarters as wages to 25 labourers, he realised a
profit of 10 quarters, which is 3 per cent. above the assumed
minimum. But if he advances 100 quarters as seed and
4 quarters each to 27 labourers, his advances will be 208 quarters, and will yield a profit less than the minimum of 7 per
cent. He will, therefore, either reduce the wages of his
27 labourers below the original rate of 4 quarters a man, or
else abandon his farm, and throw them out of employment.

In a country growing its own supplies of raw produce, not
exporting manufactured goods, and, therefore, not exposed to
foreign competition, a combination for raising wages can be

maintained only when accompanied by an auxiliary combination amongst the labouring classes for preventing the increase of their numbers. Let us proceed to consider the effect of a combination for raising wages in a country which, importing raw materials and exporting manufactured goods, is exposed to foreign competition. This is the practical, and, to the operatives of England, the vitally important branch of the subject.

In a Country depending upon Foreign Markets, Combinations for raising Wages beyond the limit determined by Foreign Competition, ultimately occasion, not an advance, but a reduction of Wages.

As before, we will assume, for the sake of illustration, that the actual rates of profit in England and in France are 10 per cent., and that, in both countries, the minimum rate of profit, without which the capitalist will not continue production, is 7 per cent. Under these circumstances, let us suppose that the operatives in England combine, and obtain such an increase of wages as will reduce the profits of their masters to the minimum of 7 per cent. In this case the English manufacturer cannot permanently reduce the price of his goods in the foreign market, because, if he did, he could not realize minimum profits. But the French manufacturer can afford to undersell the British manufacturer in the foreign market by 1, 2, or 3 per cent., and still realize his minimum profit of 7 per cent.; and, therefore, the necessary effect of the combination will be to cause the manufacturers of France to drive the manufacturers of England out of the foreign market.

Writers upon commercial policy, whose opinions are entitled to great respect, have contended that a rise of wages has no influence upon foreign trade. They maintain that a rise of wages is accompanied by a corresponding fall of profits, and does not, therefore, raise prices; and they further affirm that a fall in the rate of profit does not subject the country in which

E

it takes place to be undersold in the foreign market by other countries in which profits are higher.* The reason advanced for the doctrine, that high wages and low profits do not subject a country to any disadvantage in the foreign market is this—Should a lower rate of wages render the cost of production in France 3 per cent. higher in France than in England, and should the rate of profit be 3 per cent. higher in France than in England, the French producers might sell their goods in any foreign market 3 per cent. lower than the English producers could sell similar goods, by consenting, like the English producers, to accept a profit of 7 per cent. But it is contended that, under these circumstances, the French producers would not consent to manufacture for the foreign market at a profit of 7 per cent., for the obvious reason, that they could make 10 per cent. upon their capital in any occupation.

This argument, when stated in general terms, appears, at first sight, satisfactory; but when considered strictly and analytically, it will be seen to be wholly fallacious. The subject is so very important that it requires a detailed examination.

Let us suppose that an English and a French manufacturer have each invested 50,000*l.* in buildings and machinery, and that they each expend in a year 50,000*l.* in materials and wages. Let us also suppose that, in consequence of lower wages in France, the French manufacturer is able to employ more labourers, and to use more material than the English, and therefore fabricates, by 6 per cent. upon his floating capital, a greater quantity of goods. The goods being similar in kind and in quality, the prices obtained for them in the foreign market will be in proportion to their quantities, and the French manufacturer will sell his goods for a greater sum by 6 per cent. upon his floating capital of 50,000*l.* than the English. If the English goods sold for 57,000*l.*, the French, being greater in quantity in

* M'Culloch.

the proportion stated, would sell for 60,000*l*. Under these circumstances, would it be the interest of the French manufacturer to sell his greater quantity of goods for the same sum that the English manufacturer sold the less quantity, and thus secure a superiority in the foreign market?

When the Englishman sells his goods for 57,000*l*., he replaces his floating capital, and obtains a profit of 7 per cent., both upon his floating and upon his fixed capital; and when the Frenchman sells his goods for 60,000*l*., he replaces his advance for wages and materials, and realizes a profit of 10 per cent. upon his whole capital. Now, if the Frenchman would sell his greater quantity of goods for the same sum for which the Englishman sells the less quantity, and would be satisfied for a short time with 7 per cent. upon his original capital of 100,000*l*., he might undersell the English manufacturer and drive his goods out of the foreign market. The French manufacturer might now sell double his former quantity of goods. He might advance an additional 50,000*l*. in wages and materials, and sell the additional quantity of goods for an additional sum of 57,000*l*.; and should no additional outlay be requisite for buildings and machines, this would yield him, on his second portion of floating capital, a profit, not of 7 but of 14 per cent. It is self-evident, therefore, that if a greater quantity of materials can be worked up without an additional outlay for fixed capital, it will be the interest of the French manufacturer to take less than the average rate of profit in France upon the first portion of his advances, in order to gain more than this average rate upon the additional portions of floating capital, which he can employ by underselling the English manufacturer, and beating him out of the foreign market.

It must be apparent, that the force of this argument depends upon the fact, whether in manufacturing industry, additional floating capital can be employed without a proportionate addition of fixed capital. Now with respect to the matter of fact there can be no doubt. The market is occasionally under-stocked, and occasionally over-stocked with manufactured goods. When the supply of such goods is deficient their production is increased; and when their supply is in excess their production is diminished. But when the production of manufactured goods diminishes, the fixed capital of the manufacturer ceases to be fully employed. It is self-evident, therefore, that amid the ebbings and flowings of the market, and the alternate contractions and expansions of demand, occasions will constantly recur, in which the manufacturer may employ additional floating capital, without employing additional fixed capital. It admits of the strictest demonstration, that if additional quantities of raw material can be worked up without incurring an additional expense for buildings and machinery, the manufacturers of the country in which the rate of profit is comparatively high, will have an interest in lowering their prices in the foreign market, so as to beat out the fabrics of the country in which the rate of profit is comparatively low.

The French and English manufacturers invest each 50,000*l.* in buildings and machines, and when their fixed capital is in full action, each can employ a floating capital of 50,000*l.* in wages and raw materials. The Frenchman, paying less for labour, is able to work up more material, and produces a quantity of goods greater to the extent of 6 per cent upon his floating capital of 50,000*l.* than the quantity produced by the Englishman. The goods of each being similar in kind and quality, if those of the Englishman sell for 57,000*l.* those of the Frenchman will sell for 60,000*l.* Now it is self-evident that, under these circumstances, it would not be the interest of the French manufacturer to undersell the English, and drive him from the foreign market. For his machinery being fully employed, he cannot advance additional floating capital for wages and materials without making a proportional addition to his fixed capital; and he cannot realize 10 per cent., the customary rate of profit in France, upon his advances, unless the goods produced by a fixed capital of 50,000l., and a floating capital of 50,000l., continue to sell in the foreign market for 60,000l. He cannot therefore undersell the English manufacturer without employing additional capital in the foreign trade, at a less rate of profit than that which he might obtain in other occupations.

Very different would be the result, should a revulsion of trade check production, and prevent the fixed capital invested in manufactures from being fully employed. Let us suppose that the quantity of goods on hand is so much in excess that our manufacturers are obliged to diminish the supply, and instead of employing a floating capital of 50,000l. each, can employ floating capital of only 25,000l. each. In this case the factories will work only half time; only half the quantity of goods will be produced, and prices remaining the same,* the Frenchman's goods, instead of selling for 60,000l., will sell for only 30,000l. This will replace his floating capital of 25,000l. with a surplus of 5000l., which will amount to a profit of 6⅔ per cent. upon his whole capital of 75,000l. Under these circumstances it will be the decided interest of the French manufacturer to lower his prices, and drive the English manufacturer out of the foreign market. By doing so he will be able to employ an additional floating capital of 25,000l., without incurring an additional expense for fixed capital, and may produce an additional quantity of goods, greater by 3 per cent. than the quantity which the English manufacturer sold for 28,500l. Should he sell his greater quantity for the same sum of 28,500l., for which the English manufacturer sold his less quantity, he will drive the English manufacturer out of the foreign market, and obtain a return of 28,500l. for an advance of 25,000l. This

* Under the circumstances, prices would fall; but this, instead of weakening the case as now put, would render it still stronger.

will be a profit of 14 per cent. upon the additional floating capital employed. Now, by the supposition, the general rate of profit in France is only 10 per cent. Instead of obtaining less, the French manufacturer will gain much more than the customary rate of profit, by employing all the floating capital he can command in fabricating more goods at lower prices, and thereby expelling competitors from the foreign market.

Thus we see that the argument, so confidently advanced in support of the doctrine that a rise of wages has no injurious effect upon foreign trade is altogether erroneous, and involves the fallacy, unfortunately too prevalent amongst economical writers, of confounding distinctions by hasty generalizations, and of attributing to different things the same common properties, because we class them under the same common name.

The buildings and machines of the manufacturer, as well as the money with which he pays his wages and purchases his raw materials, are classed under the general denomination of capital; and those who, in their proneness for general reasoning, forget that science is analysis, fall into the error of conceiving that because capital, consisting of money, may pass from employment to employment, in order to obtain the customary rate of profit, capital, consisting of buildings and machinery, may be equally locomotive. The reasoning in support of the position that high comparative wages, and low comparative profits, are not injurious to foreign trade, and do not involve the danger of foreign competition, would be perfectly correct, provided fixed capital were not fixed. If money sunk in buildings and machinery could be made to realize the same customary rate of profit when the machinery is not employed as when it is employed, then indeed the manufacturers in a country in which profits were comparatively high would have no inducement to undersell the manufacturer of a country in which the customary rate of profits were low; because, in this case, the high comparative rate of profit might at all times be obtained upon the whole capital, fixed as well as floating, which the manufacturers of the high-profit country employed. But so long as buildings and machinery, when not in work, exist as dead stock, realizing no profit at all, so long will it be the interest of producers to employ, at the customary rate of profit, as much of their floating capital as possible, without reference to the consideration whether, by so employing it, they realize the customary profit upon their fixed capital also. This is a consideration which will always determine whether new and additional buildings and machines shall be erected; but when once they are erected, it will be the decided interest of the manufacturer to keep them in full work, provided he can thereby secure the customary profit upon the floating capital employed in paying wages and in purchasing raw materials. Hence, when the foreign market is overstocked, it will be the interest of the manufacturer of the high-profit country to continue to supply it at prices greatly below those ordinary prices which gave the customary return upon his whole capital, fixed and floating. This customary profit on his whole capital was necessary to induce him to *commence* business, but is not necessary to induce him to *continue* it. To secure this, it is sufficient that he obtains the customary profit upon that portion of his capital which he can transfer without loss to other occupations.

An objection may here be urged. It may be contended that the argument cuts both ways, and is as applicable to the manufacturers of the low-profit as to the manufacturers of the high-profit country. If it be the interest of the latter to continue to supply the foreign market, at prices so reduced as to leave the customary rate of profit only on the moveable portion of their capital, it must be the interest of the former to do so likewise. But if the manufacturers of the low-profit country found it their interest to continue to supply the foreign market at a reduction of prices which left them customary profits on their floating capital only, the manufacturers of the high-profit country could not undersell them without a diminution of their customary rate of profit upon that portion of their capital which they could transfer to more advantageous occupations. It follows, therefore, that a comparatively low rate of profit cannot have the effect of contracting the extent of foreign trade.

This objection proceeds upon the assumption, that prices in the foreign market never fall below that point at which the manufacturer obtains his customary rate of profit upon that portion of his capital which can be transferred without loss to other occupations; and, were this assumption conformable to fact, the objection would be valid and conclusive. But the assumption is contrary to fact. Frequent is the fall of prices below the point supposed. Revulsions occasionally occur, during which the manufacturer scarcely obtains a return sufficient to replace the floating capital he advances. Nay, in the vibrations of the market, the depression of trade will sometimes be so great that the manufacturer cannot, at existing prices, replace his floating capital, and that he continues to advance wages and materials at a positive loss, because he cannot, without incurring a greater loss, abandon his buildings and machinery; or because he is able to keep his goods on hand until the glut is removed and prices have recovered. Now, on all such occasions, the manufacturers of the high-profit country will have a decided advantage over those of the low-profit country, and will drive them out of the foreign market. Let us exemplify this process by a reference to our former case.

A French manufacturer advances a floating capital of 50,000*l.*, and produces 10,300 bales of goods; an English manufacturer also advances a floating capital of 50,000*l.*, but, as from the higher rate of wages which he pays, can employ fewer hands, and purchase less material, he produces only

10,000 bales. Under these circumstances, let us suppose that the prices of the foreign market fall so low, that the English 10,000 bales sell there for no more than 50,000*l.*, while the French 10,300 bales, of the same kind and quality, sell for a greater sum in proportion to their greater quantity, or for 51,500*l.* In this case the English manufacturer just saves himself, while the French manufacturer realizes a profit of 3 per cent. upon his floating capital.

Let us now suppose that the prices in the foreign market continue to decline, until the Frenchman's 10,300 bales, produced by a floating capital of 50,000*l.*, sell for no more than 50,000*l.*, and the Englishman's bales, produced by the same expenditure, sell for a less sum in proportion to their less quantity. In this case the Frenchman will just save himself, while the Englishman will incur a positive loss.

Thus it is self-evident, that in all revulsions of foreign trade there will be, in the country in which profits are comparatively low, a much heavier loss, and a much greater destruction of capital, than in countries in which profits are comparatively high. Should the difference in the rates of profit be considerable, the high-profit country may continue to realize moderate gains under a revulsion of foreign trade, and depression of the markets, which spread bankruptcy and ruin throughout the manufacturing districts of the low-profit country.

One other consideration remains, and it is a most important one. Floating capital has a constant tendency to transfer itself from countries in which profits are low to those in which they are high. Love of country, the inconvenience of conforming to foreign manners, and the difficulty of acquiring foreign languages, may, to a certain extent, counteract this tendency; but, notwithstanding these barriers to a perfect equalization, this tendency of profits, throughout the commercial countries of the civilized world, to gravitate towards a common level, will prevent capital from resting on those places where the cost of production has been unduly elevated. We may lay it down as a principle established by a complete induction from experience, that manufacturing industry will establish and extend itself in those countries in which manufacturing capital obtains a high comparative reward; and will partly be driven, and partly retire of its own accord, from those districts in which manufacturing profits are comparatively low.

From these illustrations, which the vital importance of the subject has led us thus to extend into demonstrative details, we can distinctly trace the ultimate effect, upon the working classes, of combinations for raising wages in a country which exports manufactured goods. In such country the price of manufactured goods in the foreign market cannot exceed the price at which they can be supplied by the foreign producer. Now, when the price of goods is thus fixed, every increase of wages, other things remaining the same, must increase the cost of production upon the domestic producer, and lower the rate of his profit; and this reduction of profit must expose him to the successful competition of those foreign manufacturing countries in which a corresponding increase of wages has not occasioned a similar fall in the rate of profit. Upon every revulsion of trade, and stagnation of the market, this fall of profits will cause the domestic producer to be undersold in the foreign market; will compel him to contract, or to discontinue his operations, and to throw his labourers partially, or wholly, out of employment. The labourers, thus thrown out, will not be able to obtain other employment at the same rate of wages as before; because, as a less quantity of manufactured goods can be exported, a less quantity of raw material and of food can be imported, and the general fund for the maintenance of labour will be diminished. Now, if the whole of the fund for the maintenance of labour, the whole quantity of food and material, be diminished, it is self-evident that, the number of labourers remaining the same, each individual must receive less real wages than before. It thus appears, by proof amounting to strictly mathematical demonstration, that in a country exporting manufactured goods, an effectual combination for increasing wages, which should have the effect of lowering the rate of profit below the rate obtained in other manufacturing countries, must ultimately terminate, not in an advance, but in a reduction of wages.

In a Country possessing superiority in manufacturing for the Foreign Markets, Wages may be raised within the limits of such superiority.

By the terms in which the important principle demonstrated in the preceding section is stated, it will be apparent that it is liable, in practice, to two exceptions. It is by increasing the cost of production, and by rendering profits comparatively low, that successful combinations for raising wages contract the field of industry, and limit foreign trade, and thus ultimately terminate in throwing labour out of employment, and in rendering wages lower than before. It follows, that, were they formed under circumstances which should prevent an increase in the cost of production, and a relative fall in the rate of profit, such combinations, instead of creating this injurious re-action, might permanently secure, to the labouring classes, a larger share of the necessaries and comforts of life. Here, then, a very important practical question arises, namely, what accompanying circumstances will prevent a rise of wages from increasing the cost of production, and from reducing the rate of profit below the rates obtained in other countries ? Let us inquire.

Should a labourer, when he demands, and obtains, an advance of wages, execute an additional quantity of work proportional to this advance, it is evident that no increase of productive cost, no decline in the rate of profit, could be thereby occasioned. If the farmer and the manufacturer paid more for labour, they would cultivate and manufacture more. The increase in their returns being in the same proportion as the increase in their advances, the cost of production, and the rate of profit, would remain the same. A greater quantity of necessaries and comforts would be produced, the fund for the maintenance of labour would be increased; and this increased fund, divided amongst the same number of individuals, would give an increased quantity of necessaries to each. It is obvious, nay, it is self-evident, that should a combination for raising wages be accompanied by an ancillary combination for increasing the hours of labour, and the quantity of work, in the same proportion in which wages might be increased, it would give to the labouring classes an increased supply of the comforts and necessaries of life. It might be difficult, it might be impracticable, to establish these co-operating combinations ; but, were they once fairly established, no injurious re-action, or recoil, could be occasioned, and wages would be permanently increased.

There is another limitation of the principle that in a country exporting manufactured goods, and importing food and raw materials, the ultimate effect of combinations for raising wages is to reduce them below the previous level. In such a country, the manner in which a compulsory elevation occasions a permanent depression of wages is by reducing the rates of profit below the rates obtained in other manufacturing countries, and thus giving to such countries a superiority in the foreign market. Now, should the particular country in which the compulsory rise of wages took place possess an advantage over other manufacturing countries in supplying the articles demanded in the foreign market, this particular country might pay high comparative wages, and yet retain its superiority with respect to foreign trade, provided the disadvantage created by the high wages were less than the advantage arising from other causes. For example, if, in fabricating a given quantity of cloth, the English manufacturer expends 100*l*. in fuel and machinery, 100*l*. in materials, and 100*l*. in wages, while the French manufacturer expends 150*l*. in fuel and machinery, 100*l*. in material, and 100*l*. in wages, then it is evident that a combination might raise wages in England from 100*l*. to 140*l*., and yet leave to England the power of underselling France in the foreign market. The disadvantage arising from the high price of labour in England would be more than counterbalanced by the advantage created by the low price of fuel and machinery. After the rise of wages, the whole cost of producing the cloth in England will be 340*l*., while in France it will be 350*l*., and the French manufacturer will still be unable to compete with the English in the foreign market. Nor would such a rise in the reward of labour be injurious to the employers of labour.

In a country which can manufacture for the foreign market at a less cost than others, a compulsory rise of wages, provided it did not go the length of equalizing productive cost, would not have the effect of reducing manufacturing profits. Under such circumstances, the price of manufactured goods would rise in the foreign market, and it would be the foreign consumer, and not the home capitalist, who would pay the advance of wages obtained by the operative class. The great value and importance of this fact will justify us in again resorting to the details of an illustrative example.

If in England and in France the cost of production were equal, and the ordinary rate of profit 10 per cent., then should the English and the French manufacturer expend each 100*l*. in fabricating and conveying a given quantity of cloth for the foreign market, in that market this quantity of cloth would sell for 110*l*. Now, suppose that in England the discovery of cheaper fuel, or an improved machine, enables the manufacturer to fabricate and convey this quantity of cloth for 90*l*., instead of for 100*l*.; then, while it continues to sell in the foreign market for 110*l.* he will realize a profit of 22 per cent. But this high rate of profit would attract capital to the business of fabricating cloth, until the increasing supply of the article so reduced its price as to leave the producer no more than the ordinary profit of 10 per cent. The quantity of cloth which had sold for 110*l.*, when its productive cost was 100*l.*, will sell for no more than 99*l.* when its cost is reduced to 90*l.* The French manufacturer would be driven out of the foreign market; but though the English manu- facturer would obtain the exclusive supplying of that market, and would consequently be able to sell a much larger quan- tity of goods than before, yet *domestic competition* would effectually prevent him from realizing a higher rate of profit than before.

Let us now suppose, that, after these effects have been produced, the operatives in England combine, and obtain an advance of wages, which raises the cost of fabricating the given quantity of cloth from 90*l.* to 98*l.*, while this quantity of cloth continues to sell in the foreign market for no more than 99*l.* This advance of wages will reduce the manu- facturer's profit from 10 to little more than 1 per cent. But capital would gradually be withdrawn from an occupation yielding so slender a return; and, even if not withdrawn from the actual fabrication of cloth, the more wealthy manu- facturers would keep their goods on hand until the diminished supply in the foreign market elevated prices, and enabled them to realize ordinary profits. The quantity of cloth which, before the rise of wages, and the consequent increased cost of production, had sold for 99*l.*, will now sell for 108*l.* in the foreign market. This rise in the price of British goods will not, however, deprive the British manufacturer of the exclusive supply of the foreign market; for by this sup- position, he is still able to undersell the French manufac- turer by nearly two per cent. But, if the British manufac- turer realizes the same rate of profit as before, and retains, as before, the exclusive supply of the foreign market, it is evident that the advance of wages obtained by the operative, must be paid by the foreign consumer, in the increased price of cloth.

Thus it appears, upon the fullest evidence, that in a country possessing a superiority over other manufacturing countries, in producing goods for the foreign market, the rate of wages may be increased above the rates obtained in other countries to nearly the whole extent of such superiority, without reducing the rate of profit, or exposing the manufacturer to foreign competition. But it will also appear, upon evidence equally conclusive, that this higher scale of wages cannot be maintained, if the operatives increase their numbers beyond the demand for labour. If, in any neighbourhood, 1000 hands are required to fabricate the goods demanded in the foreign market, and if the hands increase from 1000 to 1100, no possible combination amongst the operatives can avert a fall of wages. We have seen that all that it is possible for the most perfect combination to perform is, to increase the rate of wages to nearly the whole extent of whatever superiority the country may possess in supplying goods for the foreign market. When a rise of wages to this extent has been obtained for that number of labourers which may be required to fabricate the quantity of goods demanded in the foreign market, the price of labour cannot be further increased without losing the foreign market. But if a combination so limited the hours of labour that it required 1100 to do the work formerly done by 1000, and if each of the 1100 should receive the same wages formerly received by each of the 1000, the price of labour and the cost of production would be increased, the foreign market would be lost, and the whole of the labourers which supplied it would be thrown out of employment. If the combination should limit the hours of labour, the wages of each labourer must be reduced in proportion to the diminution in the work he performed; and should the combination, without reducing the hours of labour, limit the number of hands who should offer themselves for employment, those who were employed would have to maintain those who were unemployed, which would be the same thing in effect as a reduction of wages. To retain possession of the foreign market, and at the same time to increase the price of a given quantity of work beyond the proportion of the superiority possessed in supplying the foreign market, is manifestly impossible. But if the price of a given quantity of work cannot be increased, while the hands employed in performing it are increased, it is self-evident that the wages of each individual must be reduced. In a country possessing superiority in supplying goods for the foreign market, a combination, could it be formed and maintained, might effect an advance of wages within the limits of that superiority, provided the number of hands seeking for employment did not increase in a greater proportion than the quantity of work to be performed.*

On the manner in which limiting the time of Labour to Ten Hours would reduce Wages.

The Ten Hours Bill is objected to by many political economists as contrary to *principle,* as being at variance with the established—the cardinal doctrine of *laissez faire.* This objection is untenable. In the majority of instances in which it is put forth, the maxim, *laissez faire,* is an imitative sound, repeated with as little effort of discriminating thought as that which distinguishes

" The coxcomb bird so talkative and grave."

Governments are established for the benefit of the governed; and every species of interference on the part of the governing body, which is beneficial to any decided majority of the governed, must be a legitimate interference. The principle of non-interference can be applicable to those

* A considerable portion of the preceding pages has been taken from a tract by the same author, published several years ago, and now out of print.

circumstances only, in which interference would be productive
of mischief; in all those cases in which the interference of
the central authority in the transactions between man and
man, is capable of effecting good or averting evil, *laissez
faire* is a criminal abandonment of the functions for the
performance of which a central authority is established and
maintained. The hasty generalization which erects the
principle of *laissez faire* into an absolute truth, applicable
under all circumstances, and to be adhered to for its intrinsic
excellence, is empiricism under the guise of science.

The expediency of a Ten Hours Bill must be determined
by the self-same rules, which we have applied in determining
the expediency of combinations for raising wages. Combinations, unaccompanied by violence or intimidation, are
expedient and legitimate when their object is to raise wages
to their *maximum,* and are inexpedient and illegitimate when
they proceed a step further, and attempt to raise wages above
their *maximum.* We have seen that when wages are at their
maximum, profits are at their *minimum;* and that when
profits are at their minimum, any temporary advance of
wages must check production, diminish the demand for
labour, and thus terminate in a reduction of wages below their
former level. Analogous effects would be produced by a
Ten Hours Bill. If, in the actual state of manufacturing
industry in this country, wages are below the maximum, and
profits above the minimum, then the same wages might be
given for ten hours' labour which are now given for twelve
hours, without suspending industry and throwing the operative
out of employment; while, if wages be already at their
maximum and profits at their minimum, a diminution in the
hours of labour must inevitably lead to a corresponding
diminution in the amount of wages.

Foreign competition and foreign tariffs are progressively
depriving the British manufacturer of the superiority which
he has hitherto possessed over the foreign manufacturer.

F

Let me entreat your Lordship to consider whether, in the actual circumstances of the world, it would be possible that the British operative should continue to receive for ten hours' work the same amount of wages which he now receives for twelve hours' work. Is there a foreign market in the world to which our fabrics could be exported with a profit, were the cost of their production to be increased by the payment for the labour of ten hours, of the same amount of wages which is now paid for twelve? Let us examine this most momentous question in detail.

Our most important market is that of the United States. Under a Ten Hours Bill could this market be retained without a reduction of wages proportionate to the reduction of time? The United States possess districts of the finest coal and iron in juxtaposition, and lying near the surface; water power to an incalculable extent; indigenous supplies of cotton wool, with machinery, enterprize, and persevering industry not inferior to our own. Were America to open her ports to British fabrics, duty free, the wages of the English operative might possibly equal, but could not by possibility exceed, the wages of the American operative. But America, instead of receiving our fabrics duty free, charges a duty of 40 per cent. upon them. The price which the English manufacturer realizes for his goods in the American market, must be less by the amount of the import duty than the price which the American manufacturer realizes in the same market for the same goods. Under such circumstances it is morally impossible that the English manufacturer who supplies goods to the market of the United States, should pay to the operative an amount of wages equal to that paid by the American manufacturer. Let the hours of labour remain the same in the two countries, and the English operatives who work for the American market can continue to obtain employment only by consenting to receive an amount of wages so much below the amount received by the American operative, as may be sufficient to indemnify the English manufacturer for the duty charged by America upon British goods. Let the time of labour be ten hours in England and twelve in America, and then the English operative cannot obtain employment in working for the American market, unless he will consent, not only to receive an amount of wages reduced below the American level to an extent equivalent to the duty imposed upon British goods, but to submit to a further depression equivalent to the difference between twelve and ten. This result may be more distinctly shown by an illustrative case.

Let us suppose, as the basis of our illustration, that the rate of manufacturing profit in England is 7 per cent., and in America is 10 per cent.; that an English manufacturer and an American manufacturer have each a fixed capital of 100,000*l.* invested in buildings and machinery; that in the course of a year each works up materials to the amount of 20,000*l.*, employs 400 operatives, expends 5000*l.* in keeping his fixed capital unimpaired, produces 1000 packages of goods, and sells them in the American market for 125,000*l.* Under these assumed circumstances (and they are sufficiently analogous to actual circumstances to show the practical operation of the American tariff upon British wages), the American operative would receive 2*s.* as wages for every shilling which would be received by the English operative. The accounts of the two manufactures would stand as follows.

CASE I.

Account of the Expenditure and Return of the American Manufacturer.

EXPENDITURE.

	£.
Raw materials	20,000
Wages to 400, at 4*l.* per week, for 50 weeks,	80,000
	£100,000

F 2

RETURN.	£.
Sold 1000 packages of goods . . .	125,000
Deduct expenditure	100,000
Gross profit	25,000
Deduct replacement of fixed capital .	5,000
Net profit being 10 per cent. upon the whole capital, fixed and circulating, of 200,000*l*.	£20,000

CASE II.

Account of the Expenditure and Return of the English Manufacturer.

EXPENDITURE.	£.
Raw materials	20,000
Wages to 400, at 2*l*. per week, for 50 weeks,	40,000
	60,000

RETURN.	
Realized by the sale of 1000 packages for 125,000*l*. after payment of the duty of 40 per cent.	75,000
Deduct expenditure	60,000
Gross profit	15,000
Deduct replacement of fixed capital .	5,000
Net profit being less than 7 per cent. upon the whole, fixed and circulating capital, of 160,000*l*.	£10,000

These figures, my Lord, bring out startling results. They show that one operative in an American cotton-mill may earn an amount of wages equal to the amount which can be earned by two operatives employed in an English cotton-mill;

or, to express the same thing in other words, that an
American operative may receive for one day's work the same
amount of wages which the English operative can obtain for
two days' work.

Your Lordship will not deny that the results of these
figures are in melancholy accordance with existing facts.
They exhibit with appalling accuracy the causes of the wide
disparity which exists between the condition of the manufacturing population in England and in the United States.
Mr. Dickens has exhibited the enviable position of the factory
girls in the establishments of the Union; your Lordship has
unveiled the degradation, physical and moral, into which the
women and children employed in the establishments of
England have fallen. The contrast is humiliating and appalling. No heart which a spark of humanity ever warmed
can withhold from your Lordship the homage of respect, ap-
proval, and sympathy, for the untiring zeal and noble disregard of personal considerations, with which you have devoted
yourself to the removal of the moral plague spot from the
land, and to the performance of the Christian labour, of giving
to our manufacturing population the means of social elevation,
by securing to them a " fair day's wage for a fair day's work."
Your motives are beyond all praise. The only question is,
whether the measures which you propose would not aggravate
the evils which they are intended to remove. Let us endeavour
to solve this momentous question by tracing, through the
unerring evidence of figures, the effects which a Ten Hours'
Bill would have on the wages of the operative classes engaged
in supplying the demand of our most important foreign
market.

The expenditure and return of the American manufacturer
remains as stated in Case I. Under a Ten Hours Bill the
expenditure and return of the British manufacturer would be
as follows :—

CASE III.

Showing the Effects of a Ten Hours Bill upon the rate of profit should Wages not be reduced in those branches of Manufacture which are dependant on the Markets of the United States.

In this case the English manufacturer continues to employ a fixed capital of 100,000*l.*, and to pay 40,000*l.* in wages, while working for ten hours instead of for twelve; he expends in materials 16,667*l.* instead of 20,000*l.*; produces 833½ packages of goods instead of 1000; and obtains for them in the American market 104,167*l.* instead of 125,000*l*, which he formerly obtained for the larger quantity. His account will now stand thus:—

EXPENDITURE.

	£.
Raw materials	16,667
Wages	40,000
	56,667

RETURN.

	£.
Realized by the sale of goods to the amount of 104,167*l.*, after deducting 40 per cent. on account of duty . .	62,501
Deduct expenditure	56,667
Gross profit	5,834
Deduct for repair of fixed capital . .	5,000
Net profit, being little more than ½ per cent. upon the whole capital, fixed and circulating, of 156,667*l.* . . .	£834

The figures demonstrate, that under the operation of a Ten Hours Bill, it would be impossible that the operatives engaged in those branches of manufacture which are dependant on the markets of the United States should continue to receive the same amount of wages as at present. No Legislative enactment, no human power, can sustain wages above the amount which leaves to the capitalist a rate of profit sufficient to induce him to continue the work of production. It appeared by Case II., that while the Government of the United States continues to impose a duty of 40 per cent. upon British fabrics, profits would be below their minimum of 7 per cent., even were the English operative to receive only half the wages which are received by the American. But when profits have fallen to their minimum wages have ascended to their maximum. Force wages above the maximum and you suspend production. Enact your Ten Hours Bill and one of two events must inevitably ensue:—the manufactures of England will be transferred to foreign lands, or else the operatives must submit to a reduction of wages to the extent of 25 per cent. That a reduction of wages to this extent would be necessary, in order to enable the manufacturer to sell his fabrics in the American market at the minimum profit of 7 per cent. the following figures will serve to explain:—

CASE IV.

Showing the Effect of a Ten Hours Bill upon the Wages of the Operatives working for the American Market, under the assumption that Profits are at the Minimum of 7 per Cent.

EXPENDITURE.

	£.
Raw materials, as in Case III. . .	16,667
Wages reduced by one-fourth, or 25 per cent. below those of Case III. .	30,000
	£ 46,667

RETURN.

	£.
Proceeds of sale of goods, after deducting duty, as in Case III.	62,501
Deduct expenditure	46,667
Gross profit	15,834
Deduct replacement of fixed capital .	5,000
Net profit on fixed and circulating capital, amounting to 146,667*l*., being less than 7½ per cent.	£ 10,834

From the illustrations which I have now presented, it would appear that the effect of a Ten Hours Bill would be to cause a depression in wages, to the extent of 25 per cent., while leaving the manufacturer who supplies our most extensive and important foreign market with a rate of profit not exceeding, by ½ per cent., the minimum rate from which the slightest permanent declension would banish manufactures from the land.

Your Lordship may probably object, that the alarming conclusions at which I have thus arrived, are deduced from assumptions not in accordance with existing circumstances, and therefore not practically true; that profits are not at their minimum and wages at their maximum; and that there is still a sufficient margin to allow the operative undiminished wages for diminished work, without causing manufacturing capital to emigrate from our shores. Unfeignedly do I wish that this objection were valid. But the facts which are passing around us prove it to be groundless. Capital to an enormous amount already emigrates from our shores. Our unemployed and unemployable accumulations flow off into foreign mines and foreign loans, foreign canals, foreign railways,—foreign factories rivalling our own, have become the perennial creations of British capital. These are pre-

monitory symptoms which it would be dangerous to disregard. These are practical, undeniable, irresistible proofs,
that the rate of profit in this country is already approaching
the minimum at which no margin remains for an advance of
wages.

It is not an hypothesis, but a fact, that the wages of manufacturing labour in this country have had for a long course
of years a tendency to decline ; it is not an assumption, but
a reality, that all the principal commercial countries of the
world have adopted the policy of forcing native manufactures
by imposing increasing import duties upon British goods ; and
it is not a merely probable conclusion, but a self-evident truth,
that in the same markets commodities equal in quality will
be equal in value, and that the British manufacturer who
exports his fabrics to a foreign country, will realise for them
a less price by the amount of the import duty, than the
price realised for similar fabrics by the manufactures of that
country. Again, it is not an assumption, but a fact, that the
Anglo-Saxon race have lost nothing of their skill, and
energy, and enterprise, and persevering industry, by crossing
the Atlantic ; and it is not a merely probable inference, but
a self-evident truth, that while a day's labour in America
can produce an article equal in quantity and quality to that
produced by a day's labour in England, the maximum wages
obtainable by the American operative will exceed, in a proportion determined by the amount of duty imposed on British
goods, the maximum wages attainable by the English operative who works for the American market. And, my
Lord, it is an equally self-evident truth, that could the
wages of the operative, after the passing of your Ten Hours
Bill, be sustained for a season above the reduced maximum
determined by the diminished quantity of work, profits would
be pressed down below the minimum of continuous production, and British capital would flow out into foreign manufacturing countries in a fearfully increasing volume, leaving

your protected factory population to emigrate or to perish. I have reasoned from hypothetical cases, only for the purpose of placing before your Lordship, in a more distinct and definite form, conclusions true—self-evidently true—in the actual circumstances of society.

Perhaps your Lordship may contend, that my illustrative cases have been framed in reference to circumstances as they are found to exist in the United States exclusively; that conclusions, though necessarily true under these assumed circumstances, may not be true in reference to the different circumstances which are found to exist in the other great commercial countries of the world. I might reply, that the markets of the United States are, to the British manufacturer, the most important markets of the world; and that the ruinous consequences of a Ten Hours Bill are sufficiently demonstrated when it is shown that its operation would be, either to exclude us from the markets of the Union, or else to cause a reduction of wages proportionate to the diminution in the hours of work. But I have another and a still more conclusive answer to the objection.

The economical condition of the great commercial countries of the continent of Europe afford a perfect verification of the conclusions regarding the effect of short time upon wages, which I have presented for your consideration. The distinguishing difference between the economical condition of the United States and that of the continent of Europe, consists in the different degrees of efficacy with which labour is applied. The efficacy of labour in the United States equals, or perhaps exceeds its efficacy in England; the efficacy of labour in France is less by one-third than its efficacy in England. This difference in the efficacy of labour causes a corresponding difference in wages. An English cotton spinner produces in a day a greater quantity of yarn, and of a better quality, than a French cotton spinner; and he consequently receives more money for a

day's work than a French cotton spinner. Gold and silver
are one-third dearer, in relation to French labour and its
produce, than they are in relation to English labour and its
produce. A Frenchman labours for three weeks in executing the same quantity of work which an Englishman
executes in two weeks; and therefore the Frenchman
receives, as the wages of three weeks, no greater amount of
money than that which the Englishman receives as the
wages of two weeks. These are no theoretical conclusions
deduced from premises arbitrarily assumed ; they are existing facts, affording practical proof that the amount of wages
depends upon the quantity and value of the work performed,
and furnishing irresistible evidence- that a Ten Hours Bill
would diminish wages in the proportion in which it reduced
the number of working hours.

England's commercial rivals would rejoice and glory in
the success of your Lordship's measure for limiting the hours
of work in her factories. The commercial greatness of our
country has been created by the power which the British
operative has hitherto possessed, of executing in a given
time,—in a day or in a week,—a greater quantity of work
than that which could be executed in the same time by the
foreign operative. Remove the cause, and the effect will
cease. Diminish the quantity of work executed by the
British operative in a given time, and our commercial greatness declines. Equalize the quantity of work executed in a
day or week by the British with that executed by the foreign
operative, and England ceases to be the envy of the world.
The question of shortening the hours of labour by a legislative enactment, is the most important that can engage the
attention of the man who loves his country. May I be permitted to examine it in further detail?

Last year France imposed an additional duty upon British
yarn, and the manufacturer, in order to retain possession of
the French market, was compelled to reduce the price of the

article. France now meets the reduction of price by a further increase of duty. This will impose upon the manufacturer, if he would retain possession of the French market, another reduction of price; and the inevitable consequence. of this must be a decline of wages. And what is the remedy which you propose for averting this evil? A compulsory diminution of the hours of labour,—a legislative enactment for diminishing the quantity of work the operative may execute. You co-operate with the government of France in pulling down the greatness of England.

A large and an increasing proportion of the population of the kingdom is dependent on the demands of foreign markets for the means of subsistence. All the great commercial countries of the world have adopted the policy of forcing domestic manufactures, by imposing high import duties upon foreign fabrics. How, under such circumstances, can England hold her own? Must not British goods, when imported into a foreign country, be sold to the consumer at the same prices at which the similar goods of that country are sold to the consumer? And is it not self-evident that if British goods, upon entering the markets of a foreign country, are charged with a duty of 20, or 30, or 40 per cent., the British operative cannot receive an amount of wages equal to the amount obtained by the operatives of that country, unless he can produce in a day, or a week, a quantity of goods, greater, by 20, or 30, or 40 per cent., than the quantity produced in a day, or a week, by his foreign competitor? Your Lordship's Bill for limiting the hours of labour ought to be entitled,—" A Bill for reducing the Wages of the Operative Classes throughout the United Kingdom."

You advocate a legislative limitation of the hours of labour upon moral grounds alone, and avowedly discard all considerations of the commercial branch of this momentous question. The two branches of the subject may be separated, and perhaps conveniently separated, for the purpose of scientific disquisition; but they ought not, they cannot be separated in practical legislation. The moral and intellectual improvement of the people has an intimate, a necessary connexion with their physical well-being. Is not poverty an incentive to crime? Can the pressure of distress promote the decencies of life? Will crowded rooms and crowded beds, and contaminating associations, be prevented by a reduction of wages? Can physical degradation be the precursor of moral elevation? If these questions could be answered in the affirmative, then, indeed, the Ten Hours Bill might be discussed without reference to its effects upon the commercial prosperity of the country.

But it cannot be too often repeated that the moral and commercial branches of this important subject are incapable of separation. The two elements are held together by so close an affinity—they are so entirely incorporated and combined—they so act and react upon each other in reciprocal causation—that when we attempt to displace the one we reject an essential portion of the other. They must be dealt with as a whole—as one and indivisible. To reject the moral branch of the question would be not less fatal than to dismiss the commercial. The agitation for shortening the hours of labour in the factories involves moral considerations of the gravest character, affecting not the subjects but the promoters of the proposed legislation. The leaders of this dangerous movement bring themselves under a sacred moral obligation to tell to the working people the truth, the whole truth, and nothing but the truth. The operatives are under the delusion that, upon the passing of a Ten Hours Bill, they would receive the wages of twelve hours for the work of ten. He who, by word or by deed, by implication or by inference, should countenance this delusion, would incur an awful responsibility to the misguided people, to his country, and to his God. Look forward, I entreat you, to inevitable results. Picture to yourself what would be the state of the popular mind in the densely-peopled seats of manufacturing industry, when the masses should have awakened from their delusion, and found that your Ten Hours Bill had permanently deprived them of one-fourth part of their accustomed wages. Ask your own heart what your feelings then would be. Ask the least intelligent amongst the masses that now hail you with shouts of devoted gratitude and applause, in what degree of estimation your character would then be held.

I now conclude. Impressed with a deep conviction that, in the actual condition of this country, a legislative limitation of the hours of labour would be inexpedient and injurious in the highest degree; believing that such interference, instead of benefiting the working classes, would increase the pressure under which they are already sinking in the social scale; convinced that the increasing force of foreign competition, and the accumulating disadvantages of hostile tariffs, are the specific causes which diminish the rewards of industry in England; and regarding it as physically impossible, under the action of these causes, to improve the condition of the industrious classes, unless we can increase the efficiency of their labour, and enable them to execute a greater quantity of work within a given time:—impressed with these convictions, I have not hesitated to address to your Lordship, throughout the preceding pages, a free and unmitigated expression of my opinions in regard to a measure, the express object of which is to diminish the quantity of work performed within a given time, and of which, as I conceive, the necessary tendency would consequently be to co-operate with foreign competition and hostile tariffs in depriving British industry of the superiority which it has hitherto maintained; to effect a reduction of wages proportionate to the diminution in the quantity of work performed within a given time; and ultimately to create a bitter spirit of disappointment and despair, endangering the security of life and property, and terminating, it might be possible, in the horrors of a servile war. But while attempting to express my convictions and my apprehensions in terms of appropriate strength, it has been very far from my intention to give utterance to a word personally disrespectful to your Lordship. Your character commands respect. It is my high estimation of the moral power which that character confers which prompts this strenuous appeal. On the course which you may take in directing the popular movement incalculable consequences hang. For good or for evil, for weal or for woe, for elevating or for degrading the condition of the working classes, for advancing or for destroying the prosperity, the greatness, and the happiness of England, I regard you as a potent instrument in the hand of Providence. Will you be a rose in the garden of your country, or a thistle in her hedge? Whoever will seriously contemplate the economical condition of England must perceive that *laissez faire* is obsolete. Oil must be thrown upon the troubled waters. Unless appropriate and effectual means be adopted to mitigate the existing, the increasing pressure upon the labouring population, days of tribulation are at hand. But appropriate and effectual means for the attainment of this end are placed at our command abundantly, and only require to be skilfully, energetically, and systematically applied. Though, on the present occasion, your Lordship has overlooked these means, and mistaken the path through which the hallowed object of improving the condition of the people can be reached, yet to the self-denying zeal and unabateable perseverance with which you have struggled to achieve it, all honour and confidence are due; and though you may not immediately arrive at the conclusion that short time would be followed by a permanent reduction of wages, and by all the social ills inseparable therefrom yet I cannot but hope, I cannot but confidently believe, that the failure of your Ten Hours' Bill will cause you to seek your beneficent object through more apposite means, and to become the leader of a popular movement, the success of which, while enabling the operative to obtain advancing wages for shorter time, and while opening to the manufacturer expanding markets which hostile tariffs could not reach, would confer upon you a legitimate title to the gratitude of your country and of mankind.

I have the honour to be,
Your Lordship's most obedient servant,

R. TORRENS.

London, April 12, 1844.

Just published, by the same Author, in 1 vol. 8vo., price 10*s.* 6*d.,*

LETTERS on COMMERCIAL and COLONIAL POLICY, with an INTRODUCTION; in which the Deductive Method, as presented in Mr. Mills' System of Logic, is applied to the Solution of Controverted Questions in Political Economy.

TEN HOURS' FACTORY BILL.

THE SPEECH

OF

LORD ASHLEY, M.P.

IN THE

HOUSE OF COMMONS,

ON FRIDAY, MARCH 15th, 1844,

IN MOVING THAT THE

WORD 'NIGHT,' IN THE SECOND CLAUSE SHALL BE TAKEN TO
MEAN FROM SIX O'CLOCK IN THE EVENING TO SIX
O'CLOCK ON THE FOLLOWING MORNING.

LONDON:
JOHN OLLIVIER, PUBLISHER, 59, PALL MALL.
1844.

LONDON :
JOHN OLLIVIER, 59, PALL MALL.

SPEECH, &c.

MR. SPEAKER,

NEARLY eleven years have now elapsed since I first made the proposition to the House which I shall renew this night. Never, at any time, have I felt greater apprehension or even anxiety; not through any fear of personal defeat, for disappointment is " the badge of all our tribe ;" but because I know well the hostility that I have aroused, and the certain issues of indiscretion on my part affecting the welfare of those who have so long confided their hopes and interests to my charge.

And here let me anticipate the constant, but unjust accusation that I am animated by a peculiar hostility against factory-masters, and have always selected them as exclusive objects of attack. I must assert, that the charge, though specious, is altogether untrue. I began, I admit, this public movement by an effort to improve the condition of the factories ; but this I did, not because I ascribed to that department of industry, a monopoly of all that was pernicious and cruel ; but because it was then before the public eye, comprised the wealthiest and most responsible proprietors, and presented the greatest facilities for legislation. As soon as I had the power, I showed my impartiality by moving the House for the children's employment commission. The curious in human suffering may decide on the respective merits of the several reports ; but factory-labour has no longer an unquestionable pre-eminence of ill-fame ; and we are called upon to give relief, not because it is the *worst* system ; but because it is oppressive, and yet capable of alleviation.

B 2

Sir, I confess that ten years of experience have taught me that avarice and cruelty are not the peculiar and inherent qualities of any one class or occupation ;—they will ever be found where the means of profit are combined with great, and virtually irresponsible, power—they will be found wherever interest and selfishness have a purpose to serve, and a favourable opportunity. We are all alike, I fully believe, in the town and in the country—in manufactures and in agriculture—though we have not, all of us, the same temptations, or the same means of rendering our propensities a source of profit. And oftentimes, what we will not do ourselves, we connive at in others, if it add in any way to our convenience or pleasure. Look at the frightful records of the London dress-makers—for whom do they wear out their lives in heart-breaking toil ? Why, to supply the demands and meet the sudden and capricious tastes of people of condition ! *Here* is neither farmer nor manufacturer at fault; the scene is changed, and the responsibility too : we must ascribe it entirely to the gentler sex, and among them, not a little to our own intimacies and connexions.

And here it is just to state, that if I can recite many examples of unprincipled and griping tyranny, I can quote many also of generous and parental care, and of willing and profuse expenditure for the benefit of the people. If there are prominent instances of bad, there are also prominent instances of good men. I will suppose, for the sake of argument, that *all* are the victims, rather than the causes of the system ; but whatever the cause, the condition inflicts a great amount of physical and moral suffering. I know I am arousing a fierce spirit of reply—be it so— " Strike me, but hear me."

I shall altogether leave to others that part of the question which belongs to trade and commerce. I am neither unwilling, nor perhaps unable, to handle it ; but I desire to keep myself within the bounds that I have always hitherto observed in the discussion of this matter ; and touch only the consideration of the moral and physical effects, produced by the system, on the great body of the work-people.

I am spared, too, the necessity of arguing the propriety or impropriety of interfering to regulate the hours of labour for persons under certain ages ; the principle has long been conceded, and acted on by parliament. Our controversy can relate only to the degree in which it shall be carried out. I have never omitted an opportunity of asserting the claim I ventured to put forward nearly eleven years ago ; and I return, therefore, this evening to my original proposition.

Sir, I assume, as one ground of the argument, that, apart from considerations of humanity, which, nevertheless, should be paramount, the State has an interest and a right to watch over, and provide for, the moral and physical well-being of her people. The principle is beyond question ; it is recognized and enforced under every form of civilized government. See what is done by the powers of Europe.

Now, what has been determined by Russia in this matter? In a despatch addressed some time ago by, I think, Count Nesselrode to the then Secretary of State for Foreign Affairs of this country—the noble lord, the member for Tiverton (Lord Palmerston), this subject is alluded to, and it is stated that, " the Emperor admits the necessity of supervision—considering," says the memorandum by the Minister of Finance, " that the number of children occupied in spinning mills is likely to increase every year, the Imperial government deemed it indispensable to take such preparatory measures as will lead to legislative enactments hereafter." Then follow many regulations respecting the moral and physical treatment of the children.

In Austria, " the hours of labour are cruelly long, often fifteen, not unfrequently seventeen hours a day. The question of shortening the labour of children is under discussion." In Switzerland the regulations are very strict : " in the Canton of Argovia, no children are allowed to work, under fourteen years, more than twelve hours and a half ; and education is compulsory on the mill-owners." In the Canton of Zurich, " the hours of labour are limited to twelve ; and children under ten years of age are not allowed to be employed. The clergy are the inspectors, and the system of inspection is very rigorous." In France a bill has been framed almost on the same principles as our own, with the same restrictions. The system is, however, but imperfectly carried out on account of defective machinery; but the principle is recognised ; there are 1,200 unpaid inspectors. In Prussia, by the law of 1839, no child who has not completed his or her sixteenth year, is to be employed more than ten hours a day; none under nine years of age to be employed at all.

Now, if foreign powers consider it a matter both of duty and policy thus to interpose on behalf of their people, we, surely, should much more be animated by feelings such as theirs, when we take into our account the vast and progressively increasing numbers who are employed in these departments of industry. See how it stands. In 1818, the total number of all ages, and both sexes, employed in all the cotton factories, was 57,323. In 1835, the number employed in the five departments—cotton, woollen, worsted, flax, and silk, was 354,684. In 1839, the number in the same five departments, was 419,590; the total number of both sexes, under eighteen years of age, in the same year, was 192,887.

Simultaneously, however, with the increase of numbers has been the increase of toil. The labour performed by those engaged in the processes of manufacture, is three times as great as in the beginning of such operations. Machinery has executed, no doubt, the work that would demand the sinews of millions of men; but it has also prodigiously multiplied the labour of those who are governed by its fearful movements. I hope the house will allôw me to go through several details connected with this portion of the subject; they are technical, it is true; but, nevertheless, of sufficient importance to be brought under your attention.

In 1815, the labour of following a pair of mules spinning cotton-yarn of Nos. 40—reckoning twelve hours to the working-day—involved a necessity for walking eight miles. That is to say, the piecer, who was employed in going from one thread to another in a day of twelve hours, performed a journey of eight miles. In 1832, the distance travelled in following a pair of mules spinning cotton-yarn of the same numbers, was twenty miles, and frequently more. But the amount of labour performed by those following the mules, is not confined merely to the distance walked. There is far more to be done. In 1835, the spinner put up daily on each of these mules 820 stretches; making a total of 1,640 stretches in the course of the day. In 1832, the spinner put upon each mule 2,200 stretches, making a total of 4,400. In 1844, according to a return furnished by a practised operative spinner, the person working puts up in the same period 2,400 stretches on each mule, making a total of 4,800 stretches in the course of the day ; and in some cases, the amount of labour required is even still greater.

The House will now, probably, like to know how I have arrived at these conclusions. The calculations on which they are founded, have been made by one of the most experienced mathematicians in England. At my request he went down to Manchester, and himself made the measurements and calculation upon the spot. The measurements, I should state, were made in five different mills, spinning, respectively, yarns of the following numbers:—14, 15, 30, 38, and 40. In the mill spinning, No. 14 yarns, the least distance possible to be travelled over was seventeen miles, per day ; the greatest, possible, twenty-seven miles. In that spinning No. 15 yarns, the least distance was nineteen—the greatest twenty-nine miles. In that spinning 30, the least distance was twenty-four—the greatest thirty-seven miles. In that spinning 38, the least distance was fifteen—the greatest twenty-three miles ; but this was a machine of an old construction. In that spinning 40, the least distance was seventeen—the greatest twenty-five miles. Now, the mules which are to be followed, advance and recede—as they advance the yarn is elongated ; —and, by bearing this in mind, honourable gentlemen may see how the calculations were made. The yarn is stretched in elongated threads, and the calculations were made thus : —In the first case, the least, the assumption is, that only one thread would be broken in each movement of the mule. In the second case, that which shows the greatest amount of labour, the calculation is made upon the assumption of four threads being broken. Now, it is almost impossible that only one thread shall be broken ; and, on the other hand, it is very improbable that four threads should be in the same condition. We may, therefore, discard these extreme suppositions, and take the average of supposing two threads to be broken. On this assumption, then, the following will be the distances travelled:—In a mill spinning No. 14 yarns, twenty-two miles; No. 15 yarns, twenty-four miles; No. 30 yarns, thirty miles ; No. 38 yarns, nineteen miles (old machine); and No. 40 yarns, twenty-one miles. While these calculations were in progress, the machinery was not driven at its full speed; it might have been impelled at one-third, at least, of greater velocity.

But this is not all—there is another portion of the labour which is very oppressive, particularly to young persons—and to show its character, I will read a note made by the measurer upon the spot:—" I may also suggest that in estimating the fatigues of a day's work, due consideration should be given to the necessity of turning the body round to a reverse direction not less than from four to five thousand times in a day, besides the strain of continually having to lean over the machine and return to an erect position." The House will be aware of the great strain requisite, after leaning over the machinery, in bringing the body back to an upright position—it often happens, indeed, that the body is bent forward in the form of a right angle. Now, in the fine mills, spinning for instance No. 100 yarns, the distance travelled will be far less. It will only be 14 miles; but then the House must bear in mind that though the distance is less, the labour is equal, and in some respects greater. The exertion of leaning over the machinery is in these cases much increased, by reason of the more frequent breakages, and consequent toil in repairing them. Some of the measurements to which I have alluded were made in the mill of a gentleman named M' Connell, to whom I must express my obligation for the kindness with which he offered every facility to the gentleman who went down to the manufacturing districts for the purpose. Mr. M'Connell stood by the measurer, and made calculations simultaneously with him. At the close of the work, they compared notes; and it was found that Mr. M'Connell's measurements gave a less distance than those of the mathematician. But when they came to inquire into the reason of this difference, it was found that Mr. M'Connell had left out of his calculation all the diagonal movements. He had calculated only the straight movements, without reckoning the immense number of paces which the piecer has to make on either side. Now, these calculations are substantiated by those of several practical men. The honourable member for Oldham has himself measured in his own mill the distances travelled by the piecers ; and the results of his observations he published in a pamphlet in 1836 The distance laid down by the honourable member, is twenty miles. But I have still another authority. I submitted the case to the operative spinners of Manchester; and I have a document here, signed by twenty-two of these men, in which they state that twenty miles is the very least distance travelled, and they believe it to be still greater. I have another document sent to me in 1842, by another set of operative spinners, confirming what I have said, and stating that the labour is progressively increasing — increasing not only because the distance to be travelled is greater, but because the quantity of goods produced is multiplied, while the hands are, in proportion, fewer than before ; and moreover, because an inferior species of cotton is now often spun, which it is more difficult to work. Well, now, I know that the measurements which I have stated to the House, have been disputed by a mill-owner of great respectability—by Mr. Gregg, a very well-known gentleman, with large capital, who carries on one of the most extensive concerns of this kind in Europe. This gentleman published his contradiction to the statement which I have made, in which he estimated the distance at eight miles ; and I submitted it to the same mathematician who made the original calculation. The moment he looked at it, he said, "It is altogether inaccurate ; Mr. Gregg cannot know anything of the matter ;" and after speaking of the details, he thus sums up the question :—"Referring the matter to scientific considerations, Mr. Gregg's table must either be the result of some strange and most grievous blunderings, or of a gross perversion of observed facts, which though extremely rude and ill-chosen for the object professedly in view, could not, by any possibility, carry a fair and judicious inquiry so very far away from the truth, as to give only about one-third of the real distance." Now this is the toil imposed upon a very large portion of the population of the manufacturing districts — this is the labour imposed in the spinning-room. In the carding-room there has also been a great increase of labour—one person there does the work formerly divided between two. In the weaving room, where a vast number of persons are employed, and principally females ; an operative, writing to me, states that the labour has increased, within the last few years, fully ten per cent., owing to the increased speed of the machinery in spinning. In 1838, the number of hanks spun per week was 18,000 ; in 1843, it amounted to 21,000. In 1819, the number of picks in power-loom weaving per minute was 60—in 1842 it was 140, showing a vast increase of labour, because more nicety and attention are required to the work in hand.

Now, Sir, it is no difficult transition from such a statement of daily toil, passed as it is, in crowded rooms, heated atmospheres, noxious gases, and injurious agencies of various kinds, to the following statement of physical mischiefs to the workers employed. Since 1816, eighty surgeons and physicians, and three medical commissioners in 1833 (one of whom, Doctor Bisset Hawkins, declared that he had the authority of a large majority of the medical men of Lancashire) have asserted the prodigious evil of the system. The government commissioners themselves furnish a summary of particulars:—" The excessive fatigue, privation of sleep, pain in various parts of the body, and swelling of the feet, experienced by the young workers, coupled with the constant standing, the peculiar attitudes of the body, and the peculiar motion of the limbs required in the labour of the factory, together with the elevated temperature, and the impure atmosphere in which the labour is often carried on, do sometimes ultimately terminate in the production of serious, permanent, and incurable diseases." Doctor Loudon states—" I think it has been already proved that children have been worked a most unreasonable and cruel length of time daily, and that even adults have been expected to do a certain quantity of labour, which scarely any human being is able to endure. As a physician, I would prefer the limitation of ten hours for all persons who earn their bread by their industry." Dr. Hawkins says—" I am compelled to declare my deliberate opinion, that no child should be employed in factory labour below the age of ten, that no individual under the age of eighteen should be employed in it longer than ten hours daily." When I was myself in the manufacturing districts, in the year 1841, I went over many of the hospitals, and consulted many of the medical men in that part of the country. The result is contained in a note which I drew up at the time, and which is as follows:—" Scrofulous cases apparently universal ; the wards were filled with scrofulous knees, hips, ancles, &c. The medical gentleman informed me that they were nearly invariably factory cases. He attributed the presence of scrofula to factory employment under all its circumstances of great heat, low diet, bad ventilation, protracted toil, &c." Now the same evils are found to exist in other parts of the world where the same system is followed. A very admirable work was published a few years ago, by a

French physician, Dr. Villermé, employed by the Academie des Sciences, to examine and report upon the condition of artisans. He states, when speaking of factories in France, that " In the operations of the cotton business, cough, pulmonary inflammation, and the terrible phthisis, attack and carry off many of the work-people ; but numerous as are the victims of these disorders, their premature death seems to me less deplorable than the development of scrofula in the mass of our work-people in manufactories." Mark that: he considers death a less evil than the terrible prevalence of scrofulous disorder. Another effect produced by the system is an injurious affection of the eyesight. Any person conversant with the cotton business knows how early in life the eye is apt to become so enfeebled as scarcely to be of any effective service. There is one more fact to which I wish to call the attention of the House. Those honourable gentlemen who have been in the habit of perusing the melancholy details of mill accidents, should know that a large proportion of those accidents—particularly those which may be denominated the minor class, such as loss of fingers, and the like, occur in the last hours of the evening, when the people become so tired that they absolutely get reckless of the danger. I state this on the authority of several practical spinners.

Hence arise many serious evils to the working classes; none greater than the early prostration of their strength, their premature superannuation, and utter incapacity to sustain their families by the labour of their hands. I will prove my assertions by the following table, from which you will observe that at the very period of life at which in many other departments of industry, men are regarded as in the prime of their strength, those employed in the cotton manufacture are superannuated and set aside, as incapable of earning their livelihood by factory labour. The ages above forty are seldom found in this employment. Now during the great turn-out in 1831, from forty-two mills in Mosely, Ashton, and in other parts of Lancashire, out of 1,665 persons who joined in that turn-out, there were between forty-five and fifty years of age, only fifty-one. In 1832, it appeared by certain returns from mills in Harpur and Lanark, that out of 1,600 persons, there were above the age of forty-five, only ten individuals. In 1839, the returns from certain mills in Stockport and Manchester, showed that the number of hands employed in these mills were 22,094—Now of all that immense multitude, how many does the House suppose were above forty-five years of age? Why, only 143 persons ; and of these, sixteen were retained by special favour, and one was doing boy's work. I have in my hand, also, a list of 131 spinners made out in 1841, only seven of whom were above forty-five years of age, and almost all of these people had been refused employment. Why? Because it was declared that they were too aged for labour ! I have other authority, too, to prove the state of matters in this respect. I hold in my hand a letter from a person who went down to Bolton to make returns for me, in which he states—"I have just seen fifty reduced spinners, two are more than fifty years of age, the rest will not average forty years of age. One man, T. E., worked for sixteen years at Mr. O.'s mill ; he is forty-three years of age ; he has frequently applied for work, but is invariably answered, he is too old." The same evil exists in France and other countries where the manufacturing system prevails. Dr. Villermé says:—" There are few cities in which one meets with old people employed in manufactories, it is found to be more economical to pay younger workmen, though at a higher rate." In the year 1833, a letter was addressed to me by Mr. Ashworth, a very considerable mill-owner in Lancashire, which contains the following curious passage:—"You will next very naturally inquire about the old men, who are said to die, or become unfit for work, when they attain forty years of age, or soon after." Mark the phrase, " old man," at forty years of age ! " As all spinners, (he continues,) whether young or old, are paid the same price per pound for spinning, the production of an old man is at greater expense by reason of the diminished quantity ; this, and not ill-health, may sometimes occasion his discharge." . . . . " Old men of every description adhere to habits contracted in early life ; hence, they are troublesome to manage, and often disagree with the overlookers —this may sometimes lead to their discharge, but it appears not unfrequently that they become disinclined to work when the earnings of their families are sufficient to maintain them." Indeed ! why, there cannot, I think, be a more alarming feature in the case than the last-mentioned fact— that men, of perhaps forty, should be maintained in idleness by the labour of their families. [Loud cries of " hear, hear," from both sides of the house.] But I have the additional testimony of a government commissioner, Mr.

M'Intosh, who, in his report in 1833, says—" Although prepared by seeing childhood occupied in such a manner, it is very difficult to believe the ages of men advanced in years, as given by themselves, so complete is their premature old age." Now, Sir, I am the more inclined to rest my case with confidence on these commissioners, because they were sent expressly to collect evidence against that taken by the committee of 1832; and it is upon their reports, in considerable measure, that I will ground my appeal to this House.

Now, let this condition of things be contrasted with the condition of agricultural life; and let us see how much longer is the duration of the working powers in that class of labour. In June 1841, on an estate in Worcestershire, out of forty-two agricultural labourers, there were over forty-five years of age, twenty. Out of twenty-five on one in Lincolnshire, eleven exceeded forty years of age. At a place in Wales, out of thirty-three labourers, twelve exceeded the age of forty, and seven were above sixty. At another estate in Lincolnshire, out of sixty-two labourers, thirty-two exceeded forty years of age. At one in Scotland, out of sixty labourers, twenty-seven were over forty years of age. Again, in England, out of thirty-nine labourers, twenty-nine exceeded forty years of age. On an estate in the Isle of Wight, out of eighteen labourers, there were found ten exceeding forty years of age. On another, out of seventeen seven were above forty years of age. On another farm, out of fifteen labourers, six were over forty years of age; and, on an aggregate of farms in the neighbourhood, there were thirty labourers, every one of them exceeding forty years of age! So that the total shows, that of 341 labourers, 180 were above forty years of age. Contrast the condition of these people with that of a multitude of 22,000, of whom only 143 were above the age of forty-five. There is yet another instance. On an estate in Dorset, in 1844, out of 427 labourers, 118 are above forty-five years of age. And these men may go on much longer; for I can appeal to honourable gentlemen on both sides of the house, whether they have not known agricultural labourers, at the ages of fifty, sixty, and seventy years, still capable of working, and of earning wages.

You will, naturally enough, inquire what becomes of many of these worn out and superannuated spinners and factory hands. A few may retire to other businesses; those who have, by nature, a more vigorous mental and physical constitution, may, in some instances, survive; but a large proportion sink into a state of pauperism and decrepitude.

I hold in my hand a statement which will give the House some idea of the condition into which a vast mass of these people fall when it becomes impossible for them to earn their subsistence by factory labour. It will be borne in mind that the present system has prevailed so long, and is of such a nature as completely to have destroyed every idea of thrift and economy. The education both of males and females is such that domestic economy is almost wholly unknown to them; and it very rarely happens that they have the foresight to accumulate savings during the period at which they can work to subsist upon in the days of their old age. It will be also remembered that their strength is so wholly exhausted that they are unable to enter into any different active occupation when discharged from the mill; and that therefore they sink down into employments, of the nature of which I will give a specimen to the House. In June, 1841, from a return which was presented to me, it appeared that in 11 auction rooms in Manchester, out of 11 common jobbers, as they are called, 9 were discharged factory hands. Of 37 hawkers of nuts and oranges, 32 were factory hands; of 9 sellers of sand, 8 were factory hands; of 28 hawkers of boiled sheeps' feet, 22 belonged to the same class; of 14 hawkers of brushes, 11 were factory hands; of 25 sellers of coals, 16 were factory hands—thus out of 113 persons pursuing these miserable occupations, 89 were discharged factory hands. I may add that upon a further examination being made, it was found that of 341 discharged factory hands, 217 were maintained entirely by the earnings of their children. In Bolton, many discharged spinners were employed in sweeping the streets, and of 60 sellers of salt and gatherers of rags, 50 were factory hands. In 1842, an inquiry was made in Manchester, and it was found that of 245 cast-off spinners, there were maintained by the earnings of their children 108. The rest were following such occupations as I have already alluded to, or engaged in begging, picking up dung, and other miserable avocations. With reference to these men, I asked the question, how many may expect to be taken up on a revival of trade. The answer was, scarcely one; that the masters required young hands and unexhausted strength, and that they would rather take men of twenty-five than of thirty-five years of age—and Dr. Bisset Hawkins, one of the commissioners in 1833, gives similar testimony, that " The degree in which parents are supported by their youthful offspring at Manchester, is a peculiar feature of the place, and an unpleasing one ; the ordinary state of things in this respect is nearly reversed."

Sir, neither the existence, nor the consequences, of these destructive causes, have escaped the attention of continental writers and legislators. Their testimonies and their laws strongly confirm the opinions and statements of those, who, in this country, have so long urged, upon the public consideration, the perilous necessity of withstanding the further progress of such pernicious agencies. By the system we permit, the laws of nature are absolutely outraged, but not with impunity. The slow but certain penalty is exacted in the physical degradation of the human race, including, as it does, the ruin of the body, and the still more fatal corruption of the moral part.

In the year 1840, a commission was issued in France. A report was made to the French Chamber of Peers, by M. Dupin, the Baron Charles Dupin, and to that eminent person I am indebted for the copy of the report from which are taken the extracts to which I am about to refer. I hope the House will attend to the facts adduced by this gentleman.

" We were desirous," says the reporter, " of ascertaining the amount of difference in force and physical power, between the parties which have respectively attained the age of manhood in the parts of France most devoted to agriculture, and those where manufacturing industry is more generally diffused. The councils of revision in the recruiting department exhibited the following facts :—For 10,000 young men capable of military service, there were rejected as infirm, or otherwise unfit in body, 4,029 in the departments most agricultural : for 10,000 in the departments most manufacturing, there were rejected 9,930." The reporter then proceeds to speak in detail. " There were found," he says, " for 10,000 capable of military service, in Marne, 10,309 incapable ; in the Lower Seine, 11,990 incapable ; in L'Eure, 14,450 incapable." Now what is the comment of the reporter on this? I will take the liberty of reading it to the House, because of the solemn warning it conveys to all governments and nations. " These deformities," he proceeds, " cannot allow the legislature to remain indifferent ; they attest the deep and painful mischiefs—they re-
10

veal the intolerable nature of individual suffering; they
enfeeble the country in respect to its capacity for military
operations, and impoverish it in regard to the works of
peace. We should blush for agriculture, if, in her operations, she brought, at the age adapted to labour, so small
a proportion of oxen or horses in a fit state for toil with so
large a number of infirm and misshapen." Now, this is a
return which I have once before quoted ; but I quote it
again, because it is so singularly adapted to our present
position. We have no means of applying to our population the same test as that in France, because we have not
the same courts for examination into the ability of people
to carry arms; but if such tribunals existed, I fear that
they would set forth results far more distressing. If, for
the comparatively short time that manufactures have been
established in France, such terrible results are exhibited,
what must be the case in England, where they have prevailed
for considerably more than half a century? Just see what Dr.
Villermé says. Dr. Villermé, having enlarged on the pernicious effects of factory labour, adds :—" In examining
men from twenty to twenty-one years of age, I found them
physically unfit for the military service in proportion as
they came from the working classes of the factory (*classe
ouvrière de la fabrique*) at Amiens. 100 fit men required
193 conscripts from the middling class ; 100 fit men required 343 conscripts from the working class."
 Is this all? By no means—we have, if possible, yet
stronger testimony from Prussia. The sovereign of that
country thought fit to enforce a law of protection, for all
under sixteen years of age, against more than ten hours'
labour in the course of the day. What was the reason
assigned ?—here is the document !
 From the Official Gazette of Laws, 9th March 1839.
 " ' His Majesty was pleased to direct the attention of his
ministers to a report from Lieutenant George Von Horn,
that the manufacturing districts would not fully supply
their contingents for the recruiting of the army, that the
physical development of persons of tender years was
checked, and that there was reason to believe, that in
the manufacturing districts, the future generations would
grow up weaker and more crippled than the existing one
was stated to be—employed from eleven to fourteen hours
daily, in excessive labour, frightfully disproportioned to
the powers of persons from eight to eighteen years of

age." Then followed an inquiry very similar to our own, which fully confirmed every statement; and the document proceeds—" The preceding facts show that urgent necessity for legislative interference felt by the King to put a stop to such premature, unnatural, and injurious employment of the young operatives in factories."

I need not detain the house by an endeavour to show, that similar or worse mischiefs must have arisen in our own country—I speak of those districts only where the manufacturing system has long and extensively prevailed ; I know that the agricultural parts and hilly regions of Yorkshire and Lancashire still send forth a noble race of human beings. But let me here impress upon the House the necessity of deeply considering these important statements. The tendency of the various improvements in machinery is to supersede the employment of adult males, and substitute in its place, the labour of children and females. What will be the effect on future generations, if their tender frames be subjected, without limitation or control, to such destructive agencies?

Consider this; in 1835, the numbers stood thus; the females in the five departments of industry, 196,383 ; in 1839, females, 242,296; of these, the females under 18, 112,192. The proportions in each department stood, females in cotton, 56¼ per cent. ; ditto worsted, 69½ ditto ; ditto silk, 70½ ditto; ditto flax, 70½ ditto. Thus while the total amount of both sexes and all ages, in the cotton manufacture, in 1818, were equal only to 57,323, the females alone in that branch, in 1839, were 146,331. Now the following is an extract of a letter from a great mill-owner in 1842 :—" The village of —— two miles distant, sends down daily to the mills in this town, at least a thousand females, single and married, who have to keep strictly the present long hours of labour. Seven years ago, these persons were employed at their own homes; but now, instead of the men working at the power-looms, none but girls or women are allowed to have it." But, Sir, look at the physical effect of this system on the women. See its influence on the delicate constitutions and tender forms of the female sex. Let it be recollected that the age at which the "prolonged labour," as it is called, commences, is at the age of 13. That age, according to the testimony of medical men, is the tenderest period of female life. Observe the appalling progress of female labour ; and remember that the

c

necessity for particular protection to females against over-work is attested by the most eminent surgeons and physicians —Dr. Blundell, Sir Anthony Carlisle, Sir William Blizard, Dr. Elliotson, Sir George Tuthill, Sir Benjamin Brodie, John Henry Green, Esq., of Saint Thomas's, Charles Aston Key, Esq., George James Guthrie, Esq., Mr. Travers, Sir Charles Bell, Dr. Hodgkin, John Morgan, Esq., of Guy's Hospital, Samuel Smith, Esq., surgeon, of Leeds, Doctor Young of Bolton, John Malyn, Esq., Peter Mark Roget, Esq., some time physician to the Manchester Infirmary. Here are some specimens of their evidence:—" Is it not especially necessary to give protection from excessive labour to females when approaching the age of puberty ? —Quite important, if they are afterwards to become mothers, quite essential;" this is an universal opinion. Many anatomical reasons are assigned by surgeons of the manufacturing towns, that "the peculiar structure of the female form is not so well adapted to long-continued labour, and especially labour which is endured standing." Mr. Smith, of Leeds, declares:—" This (the operation of the factory labour) occasionally produces the most la-mentable effects in females, when they are expecting to become mothers." On the anatomical difficulty of partu-rition, he states—" It is often the painful duty of the accoucheur to destroy the life of the child. I have seen many instances of the kind, all of which, with one single exception, have been those of females who have worked long hours in factories." "There is a foundation in nature," says Dr. Blundell, " for the customary division which assigns the more active labour to the male, and the sedentary to the female"—" among savages, the woman is often the drudge." George James Guthrie, Esq. : " Have you not been a medical officer in the armies of this country for a considerable length of time ?—Yes. Would you sanction, for a continuance, soldiers being actually under arms for twelve hours a day for a succes-sion of days?—Such a thing is never done nor thought of ; a soldier is never kept under arms more than five or six hours, unless before the enemy. Is the female sex well fitted to sustain long exertion in a standing posture ? It is not. Is it not more than ordinarily necessary to pro-tect females against excessive labour, when approaching the age of puberty ?—Certainly it is." " The ten hours," he adds, " you propose to give to the children in factories, is the work you would not give to soldiers, even when soldiers are employed in public works ; they would not then be worked more than twelve hours, granting them time for their meals ; and for the work they would have additional pay."

Now, Sir, mark the fearful superseding of adult workers; " the tendency of improvements in machinery," say all the inspectors, " is more and more to substitute infant for adult labour." Dr. Villermé, in his *Tableau d'état physique et moral des ouvriers,* urges the same results that " children and women are employed instead of men." In one mill (1831) adults, 70 ; spindles to each, 104 ; piecers, 305. In same mill (1841) adults, 26 ; spindles to each, 223 ; piecers, 123 ; being one-sixth, instead of one-fifth, as before, of the hands employed. In Bolton (1835) thirty-nine mills set up 589,784 spindles ; the same mills set up (1841) 740,000 spindles ; piecers to these spindles—(1835), 2,443 ; ditto in 1841, 2,426 ; spinners to them in 1835, 797 ; ditto in 1841, 727. Observe, too, the process of double-decking and self-actors —In 1831, twenty-three mills employed 1,267 spinners (Manchester) ; in 1839, the same twenty-three mills employed 677 spinners ; thus throwing out 590 spinners, without any abatement of productive power. In 1829, in Manchester, spinners, 2,650 : 1841, in Manchester, spinners, 1,037 ; thrown out entirely, 1,613. In 1835, 2,171 spinners worked 1,229,204 spindles ; in 1841, 1037 spinners worked 1,431,619 spindles. Observe, too, that the labour is greatly increased upon children in all mills alike. In 1829, in the mill of Mr. ——— ; spinners, 70 ; spindles worked, 43,680; piecers, 230. In 1841, in same mill, spinners, 26 ; spindles, 43,796 ; piecers, 134. In 1829, in a mill, spinners, 53 ; spindles, 23,800 ; piecers, 125. In 1842, spinners, none ; spindles, same number ; piecers, 84. In 1829, in thirty-five mills, spinners, 1,088 ; spindles, 496,942. In 1841, in same mills, spinners, 448 ; spindles, 556,375 ; self-actors, 473, wrought by children and young persons only. A working spinner makes this statement, and it is a fair sample of the whole : " My wheels are trebled ; the piecers reduced to eight ; thus, two do the work of three. ' Self-acting greatly augments labour by the increased velocity of the machine, and the greater number of spindles apportioned to each piecer."

Here, Sir, pause to consider the multitudes of females on

whom this system must exercise its influence, and their great increase since 1835. "Mr. Orrell's mill," says the inspector, and I will quote this as an example, " at Heaton Norris, is by far the largest in Stockport. We are employing (says Robert M'Lure, the manager) altogether, in that mill, and in connection with it (as carters, gas-men, and others), 1,264 hands at this time, of whom 846 are females. The whole number of looms is 1,300, all standing on one flat, attended by 651 females, and twenty-one males." But there is a reason for this substitution ; I will show, by an extract from a letter dated in March 1842, the motives that actuate some minds :—" Mr. E., a manufacturer, (says the writer,) informed me that he employs females exclusively at his power-looms ; it is so universally; gives a decided preference to married females, especially those who have families at home dependent on them for support ; they are attentive, docile, more so than unmarried females, and are compelled to use their utmost exertions to procure the necessaries of life."

Thus, Sir, are the virtues, the peculiar virtues, of the female character to be perverted to her injury—thus all that is most dutiful and tender in her nature is to be made the means of her bondage and suffering ! But consider again, I entreat you, what a multitude of females it is on whom this system has its operation. Just survey the enormous increase since 1835. This is the further testimony of the Sub-inspector Baker, in his report of 1843. There are employed in his district more than in 1838, 6,040 persons ; of these, 785 males ; 5,225 females. " The small amount of wages," says the Inspector Saunders, " paid to women, acts as a strong inducement to the mill-occupiers to employ them instead of men, and in power-loom shops this has been the case to a great extent." Now hear how these poor creatures are worked. Mr. Baker reports, as to " having seen several females, who, he was sure, could only just have completed their eighteenth year, who had been obliged to work from six A. M. to ten P. M., with only one hour and a-half for meals. In other cases, he shows, females are obliged to work all night, in a temperature of from 70 to 80 deg. Hence Mr. Saunders (1843) deduces the necessity of a law protecting all females, up to the age of twenty-one ; adding, medical men invariably declare the urgent necessity of protecting from excessive labour all females up to that period of life. I found (says Mr. Horner, October 1843) many young women, just

eighteen years of age, at work from half-past fiv
morning until eight o'clock at night, with no ces
cept a quarter of an hour for breakfast, and three qua
of an hour for dinner. They may fairly be said to labour
for fifteen hours and a-half out of twenty-four. There are
(says Mr. Saunders) among them, females who have been
employed for some weeks, with an interval only of a few
days, from six o'clock in the morning until twelve o'clock
at night, less than two hours for meals, thus giving them
for five nights in the week, six hours out of its twenty-four
to go to and from their homes, and to obtain rest in bed."
" A vast majority," says Mr. Saunders, in January 1844,
" of the persons employed at night, and for long hours
during the day, are females; their labour is cheaper, and
they are more easily induced to undergo severe bodily
fatigue than men."

Where, Sir, under this condition, are the possibilities of
domestic life? how can its obligations be fulfilled? Regard
the woman as wife or mother, how can she accomplish any
portion of her calling? And if she cannot do that which
Providence has assigned her, what must be the effect on
the whole surface of society? But to revert to the physical effects—Mr. Saunders says in the same report, "The
surgeon distinctly condemns such employment; though the
effect may not be immediately apparent, it must have a tendency to undermine the constitution, produces premature decay, and shortens the duration of human life. No
female," he adds, " ought to work more than ten hours, and
that twelve hours produces severe injury to those in a state
of pregnancy;" he often witnesses the effect of so much
standing when parturition comes on; adding, " work in the
night is the most injurious; it is unnatural, and not adapted
to the constitution of women." Another surgeon, of great
experience, in Lancashire, writes to me that, " after thirteen is the age when young women begin to be most suscep-
tible of injury from factory work," and much more at this
period of their lives " than at the earlier ages." He proceeds to details : " the effects of long-continued labour in
factories become more apparent after childbirth. The infants are at birth below the average size, have a stinted,
shrivelled appearance. I would take a score of factory
births, and the same of healthy parents, and distinguish
between them." Children are much confined by factory mothers to care of others—opium administered to the infants

in various forms—the quantity of this pernicious drug thus consumed would almost stagger belief—many infants are so habituated to it, that they can scarcely exist when deprived of the stimulus—immense numbers fall victims. to hydrocephalus—mothers' milk becomes deteriorated—infants fed upon substitutes in her absence—hence internal disorders, of which the usual remedy is gin." "Miscarriages very frequent, and all the physical and surgical mischiefs of mistreated pregnancy—varicose veins produced by the continued evil practice—aggravated greatly in pregnant women." "Again, troublesome ulcers of the legs, arising from varicose veins, which, in some cases, burst, and bring on a dangerous and sometimes fatal hæmorrhage." "The practice of procuring abortion is very frequent, even among married women." I have, moreover, the personal testimony of several females to the truth of these statements—they speak of the intolerable pain in their breasts by such long absences from children, and the suffering of returning to work within ten days of confinement."

Look again to the effects on domestic economy; out of thirteen married females taken at one mill, only one knew how to make her husband a shirt, and only four knew how to mend one. I have the evidence of several females, who declare their own ignorance of every domestic accomplishment:—The unmarried declare, "not a single qualification of any sort for household servants." The married; "untidy, slovenly, dirty; cannot work, sew, take care of children, or the house; cannot manage expenses; perpetual waste and extravagance." But hear the history of their daily life from their own lips:—

"M. H., aged twenty years, leaves a young child in care of another, a little older, for hours together; leaves home soon after five, and returns at eight: during the day the milk runs from her breasts until her clothes have been as wet as a sop." M. S. (single) leaves home at five, returns at nine: her mother states she knows nothing but mill and bed; can neither read, write, knit, nor sew. H. W. has three children: leaves home at five on Monday; does not return till Saturday at seven: has then so much to do for her children, that she cannot go to bed before three o'clock on Sunday morning. Oftentimes completely drenched by the rain, and has to work all day in that condition. "My breasts have given me the most shocking pain, and I have been dripping wet with milk." I will conclude this part with an extract

from a letter, dated February 1840, by Dr. Johns, Superintendent Registrar of the Manchester district : an important document, when we consider that it was written to
controvert some of my statements respecting the mortality
of those districts. "Very young children," says Dr.
Johns, "are, by the existing system, not sufficiently taken
care of by their mothers: as regards themselves, during
gestation, and their offspring, after childbirth—the women,
during pregnancy, continue as long as possible at their
work ; and sooner than they ought, they again attend the
factories, leaving their infants to the care of ill-paid and
unsuitable persons, to take the oversight of the children in
their absence; nor ought we to omit that soothing drugs—
the well-known nostrum—Godfrey's cordial, are often had
recourse to, with a view to lull the troubles of the little
unfortunates, and hence, perhaps, may be attributable to
the improper use of narcotics, the frequent deaths from con-
vulsions. It is most desirable that mothers should not be,
if possible, abstracted from their attention to their helpless
infants, certainly not during the period of lactation and
teething."

So much, Sir, for their physical, and, if I may so speak,
their financial condition : the picture of their moral state
will not be more consolatory. And, first, their excessive
intemperance :—

Mr. Roberton, a distinguished surgeon at Manchester,
says, in a published essay, "I regard it as a misfortune for
an operative to be obliged to labour for so long hours at an
exhausting occupation, and often in an impure atmosphere.
I consider this circumstance as one of the chief causes of
the astounding inebriety of our population." I read in a
private letter from Manchester, 1843 : "Intemperance is
making progress; on Sundays there is more drinking than
there has been for many years; the people who sell ale,
&c., state to me that they never sold more on Sunday, nor
as much as they now do." Mr. Braidley, when borough-
reeve of Manchester, stated, that in one gin shop, during
eight successive Saturday evenings, from seven till ten
o'clock, he observed, on an average rate, 412 persons enter
by the hour, of which the females were 60 per cent."
Many females state, that the labour induces "an intolerable thirst ; they can drink, but not eat." I do not doubt
that several of the statements I have read, will create sur
prise in the minds of many honourable members ; but if

they were to converse with operatives who are acquainted with the practical effects of the system, they would cease to wonder at the facts I have detailed. I might detain the House by enumerating the evils which result from the long working of males and females together in the same room. I could show the many and painful effects to which females are exposed, and the manner in which they lament and shrink from the inconveniences of their situation. I have letters from Stockport and Manchester, from various individuals, dwelling on the mischievous consequences which arise from the practice of modest women working so many hours together with men, and not being able to avail themselves of those opportunities which would suggest themselves to every one's mind without particular mention. Many mills, I readily admit, are admirably regulated, but they are yet in a minority—were all of such a description as several that I have seen, they might not, perhaps, require any enactments. But to return.—Mr. Rayner, the medical officer of Stockport, says:—" It has been the practice in mills, gradually to dispense with the labour of males, but particularly grown-up men, so that the burden of maintaining the family has rested almost exclusively on the wife and children, while the men have had to stay at home, and look after household affairs, or ramble about the streets unemployed." But listen to another fact, and one deserving of serious attention; that the females not only perform the labour, but occupy the places of men; they are forming various clubs and associations, and gradually acquiring all those privileges which are held to be the proper portion of the male sex. These female clubs are thus described :—" Fifty or sixty females, married and single, form themselves into clubs, ostensibly for protection; but, in fact, they meet together to drink, sing, and smoke; they use, it is stated, the lowest, most brutal, and most disgusting language imaginable." Here is a dialogue which occurred in one of these clubs, from an ear-witness :—" A man came into one of these club-rooms, with a child in his arms; 'Come lass,' said he, addressing one of the women, ' come home, for I cannot keep this bairn quiet, and the other I have left crying at home.' ' I won't go home, idle devil,' she replied, ' I have thee to keep, and the bairns too, and if I can't get a pint of ale quietly, it is tiresome. This is the only second pint that Bess and me have had between us; thou may sup if thou likes, and sit thee down, but I won't go home yet.' "

Whence is it that this singular and unnatural change is taking place? Because that on women are imposed the duty and burthen of supporting their husbands and families, a perversion as it were of nature, which has the inevitable effect of introducing into families disorder, insubordination, and conflict. What is the ground on which the woman says she will pay no attention to her domestic duties, nor give the obedience which is owing to her husband? because on her devolves the labour which ought to fall to his share, and she throws out the taunt, " If I have the labour, I will also have the amusement." The same mischief is taking place between children and their parents; the insubordination of children is now one of the most frightful evils of the manufacturing districts. " Children and young persons take the same advantage of parents that women do of their husbands, frequently using oaths and harsh language, and, if corrected, will turn round and say, " ———— you, we have you to keep." One poor woman stated that her husband had chided two of their daughters for going to a public-house; he made it worse, for they would not come home again, stating, 'they had their father to keep, and they would not be dictated to by him.'" This conduct in the children is likewise grounded on the assertion that the parents have no right to interfere and control them, since, without their labour, the parents could not exist; and this is the bearing of children, many of whom are under thirteen or fourteen years of age! Observe carefully, too, the ferocity of character which is exhibited by a great mass of the female population of the manufacturing towns. Recollect the outbreak of 1842, and the share borne in that by the girls and women; and the still more frightful contingencies which may be in store for the future. " I met," says an informant of mine, " with a mother of factory workers, who told me that all the churches and chapels were useless places, and so was all the talk about education, since the young and old were unable to attend, either in consequence of the former being imprisoned in the mills so many hours, and being in want of rest the little time they were at home; and the latter being compelled to live out of the small earnings of their children, and cannot get clothing, so they never think of going to churches or chapels. She added, ' when you get up to London, tell them we'll turn out the next time (meaning the women), and let the soldiers fire upon us if they dare, and depend upon it there will be a break out, and a right one, if that House of Commons don't alter things, for they can alter if they will, by taking mothers and daughters out of the factories, and sending the men and big lads in.'" But further, what says Sir Charles Shaw, for some years the superintendent of the police of Manchester—what is his opinion of the condition of the females of that town, and the effects produced, by the system under which they live, on their conduct and character?—"Women," says he, "by being employed in a factory, lose the station ordained them by Providence, and become similar to the female followers of an army, wearing the garb of women, but actuated by the worst passions of men. The women are the leaders and exciters of the young men to violence in every riot and outbreak in the manufacturing districts, and the language they indulge in is of a horrid description. While they are themselves demoralized, they contaminate all that comes within their reach."

This will conclude the statement that I have to make to the House,—and now, Sir, who will assert that these things should be permitted to exist? Who will hesitate to apply the axe to the root of the tree, or, at least, endeavour to lop off some of its deadliest branches? What arguments from general principles will they adduce against my proposition? What, drawn from peculiar circumstances? They cannot urge that particular causes in England give rise to particular results; the same cause prevails in various countries; and wherever it is found, it produces the same effects. I have already stated its operation in France, in Russia, in Switzerland, in Austria, and in Prussia; I may add also in America: for I perceive by the papers of the first of February, that a bill has been proposed in the legislature of Pennsylvania to place all persons under the age of sixteen, within the protection of the " ten hours " limit. I never thought that we should have learned justice from the city of Philadelphia. In October last, I visited an immense establishment in Austria, which gives employment to several hundred hands; I went over the whole, and conversed with the managers, who detailed to me the same evils and the same fruits as those I have narrated to the House—prolonged labour of sixteen and seventeen hours, intense fatigue, enfeebled frames, frequent consumptive disorders, and early deaths—yet the locality had every advantage; well-built and airy houses, in a fine open country, and a rural district;

nevertheless, so injurious are the effects, that the manager added, stating at the same time, the testimony of many others who resided in districts where mills are more abundant, that, in ten years from the time at which he spoke, "there would hardly be a man in the whole of those neighbourhoods fit to carry a musket." Let me remind, too, the House, of the mighty change which has taken place among the opponents to this question. When I first brought it forward in 1833, I could scarcely number a dozen masters on my side, I now count them by hundreds. We have had, from the West Riding of Yorkshire, a petition signed by three hundred millowners, praying for a limitation of labour to ten hours in the day. Some of the best names in Lancashire openly support me. I have letters from others who secretly wish me well, but hesitate to proclaim their adherence; and even among the members of the Anti-Corn-Law League, I may boast of many firm and efficient friends.

Sir, under all the aspects in which it can be viewed, this system of things must be abrogated or restrained—it affects the internal tranquillity of those vast provinces, and all relations between employer and employed—it forms a perpetual grievance, and ever comes uppermost among their complaints in all times of difficulty and discontent. It disturbs the order of nature, and the rights of the labouring men, by ejecting the males from the workshop, and filling their places by females, who are thus withdrawn from all their domestic duties, and exposed to insufferable toil at half the wages that would be assigned to males, for the support of their families.

It affects—nay, more, it absolutely annihilates, all the arrangements and provisions of domestic economy—thrift and management are altogether impossible; had they twice the amount of their present wages, they would be but slightly benefited—everything runs to waste; the house and children are deserted; the wife can do nothing for her husband and family: she can neither cook, wash, repair clothes, or take charge of the infants; all must be paid for out of her scanty earnings, and, after all, most imperfectly done. Dirt, discomfort, ignorance, recklessness, are the portion of such households; the wife has no time for learning in her youth, and none for practice in her riper age; the females are most unequal to the duties of the men in the factories; and all things go to rack and ruin, because the men can discharge at home no one of the especial duties that providence has assigned to the females. Why need I detain the House by a specification of these injurious results? They will find them stated at painful length in the Second Report of the Children's Employment Commission.

Consider it, too, under its physical aspect! Will the House turn a deaf ear to the complaints of suffering that resound from all quarters? Will it be indifferent to the physical consequences on the rising generation? You have the authority of the government commissioner, Dr. Hawkins, a gentleman well skilled in medical statistics—"I have never been," he tells you, "in any town in Great Britain or in Europe, in which degeneracy of form and colour from the national standard has been so obvious" as in Manchester. I have, moreover, the authority of one of my most ardent antagonists, himself a mighty millowner, that, if the present system of labour be persevered in, the "county of Lancaster will speedily become a province of pigmies." The toil of the females has hitherto been considered the characteristic of savage life; but we, in the height of our refinement, impose on the wives and daughters of England a burden from which, at least during pregnancy, they would be exempted even in slaveholding states, and among the Indians of America.

But every consideration sinks to nothing compared with that which springs from the contemplation of the moral mischiefs this system engenders and sustains. You are poisoning the very sources of order and happiness and virtue; you are tearing up, root and branch, all the relations of families to each other; you are annulling, as it were, the institution of domestic life, decreed by Providence himself, the wisest and kindest of earthly ordinances, the mainstay of social peace and virtue, and therein of national security. There is a time to be born, and a time to die —this we readily concede; but is there not also a time to live, to live to every conjugal and parental duty?—this we seem as stiffly to deny; and yet in the very same breath we talk of the value of education, and the necessity of moral and religious training. Sir, it is all in vain, there is no national, no private system, that can supersede the influence of the parental precept and parental example—they are ordained to exercise an unlimited power over the years of childhood; and, amidst all their imperfections, are accom-

8

panied with a blessing. Whose experience is so confined that it does not extend to a knowledge and an appreciation of the maternal influence over every grade and department of society? It matters not whether it be prince or peasant, all that is best, all that is lasting in the character of a man, he has learnt at his mother's knees. Search the records, examine the opening years of those who have been distinguished for ability and virtue, and you will ascribe, with but few exceptions, the early culture of their minds, and above all, the first discipline of the heart, to the intelligence and affection of the mother, or at least of some pious woman, who, with the self-denial and tenderness of her sex, has entered, as a substitute, on the sacred office. No, Sir, these sources of mischief must be dried up; every public consideration demands such an issue; the health of the females; the care of their families; their conjugal and parental duties; the comfort of their homes; the decency of their lives; the rights of their husbands; the peace of society; and the laws of God;—and, until a vote shall have been given this night, which God avert, I never will believe that there can be found in this house one individual man who will deliberately and conscientiously inflict, on the women of England, such a burthen of insufferable toil.

Sir, it is very sad, though perhaps inevitable, that such weighty charges and suspicions should lie on the the objects of those who call for, and who propose, this remedial measure. I am most unwilling to speak of myself; my personal character is, doubtless, of no consequence to the world at large; but it may be of consequence to those whose interests I represent; because distrust begets delays; and zeal grows cold, when held back in its career by the apprehension that those, whom it would support, are actuated by unworthy motives. Disclaimers, I know, are poor things when uttered by parties whom you listen to with suspicion or dislike; but consider it calmly; are you reasonable to impute to me a settled desire, a single purpose, to exalt the landed, and humiliate the commercial aristocracy? Most solemnly do I deny the accusation; if you think me wicked enough, do you think me fool enough, for such a hateful policy? Can any man in his senses now hesitate to believe that the permanent prosperity of the manufacturing body, in all its several aspects, physical, moral, and commercial, is essential, not only to the welfare, but absolutely to the existence of the British empire? No, we fear not the increase of your political power, nor envy your stupendous riches; " peace be within your walls, and plenteousness within your palaces !" We ask but a slight relaxation of toil, a time to live, and a time to die; a time for those comforts that sweeten life, and a time for those duties that adorn it;—and, therefore, with a fervent prayer to Almighty God that it may please him to turn the hearts of all who hear me to thoughts of justice and of mercy, I now finally commit the issue to the judgment and humanity of parliament.

LONDON :

JOHN OLLIVIER, 59, PALL MALL.

TEN HOURS FACTORY BILL.

THE SPEECH

OF

LORD ASHLEY, M.P.,

IN THE HOUSE OF COMMONS

ON

FRIDAY, 10TH MAY, 1844,

ON MOVING

" That the Clause (And be it Enacted, That from and after the 1st day of
October in the present year, no young person shall be employed in any
Factory more than eleven hours in any one day, or more than sixty-four
hours in any one week; and that from and after the 1st day of October
1847, no young person shall be employed in any Factory more than ten
hours in any one day, or more than fifty-eight hours in any one week; and
that any person who shall be convicted of employing a young person for
any longer time than is in and by this Clause permitted, shall for every
such offence be adjudged to pay a penalty of not less than £   , and not
more than £), be now read a second time."

LONDON:

JOHN OLLIVIER, 59, PALL MALL.

1844.

Much uncertainty having prevailed respecting the extent of Lord Ashley's Amendment, it is necessary to state, that the term "young person," is taken according to the definition of the Factory Act, and is applicable to all between the ages of 13 and 18.

SPEECH, &c.

It may seem to be almost superfluous, after three distinct declarations of this House, (and in a single session,) to appeal again, by rhetoric or argument, to your feelings or understanding. We determined only seven weeks ago, three times actually, that the period of labour should be less than twelve hours; and twice virtually, that it should not exceed ten. The world at large believed that a middle term would be offered; but her Majesty's Ministers have refused concession—they have invited, nay more, have compelled us to revive the debate; and now summon the House of Commons to revoke its decision. We, then, who stand in the old paths, and protest against this novel and somewhat questionable course, shall not be regarded as guilty of wearying your attention, and wasting your time, if we urge every possible consideration, and press forward every hitherto-omitted argument, as some counterpoise to the enormous weight of ministerial influence and official authority.

Sir, I cannot but be aware that enough has been said on the physical and social condition of the people—one way or the other, the minds of all are fully made up; and it is, indeed, unnecessary to say more, as all, even the hottest of my opponents, admit that a reduction of the hours of labour, could it be effected without injury to the workmen and manufacturers, would be highly desirable. The only objection, then, in the minds of many honourable and thinking men, is the danger to the people themselves; and I find myself in the condition of being summoned to refute the charge, that I, who propose the scheme, am far more inhuman than those who resist it. Now I, for one, will reject the use of such epithets as these; nor will I retort any accusations that, here or elsewhere, have cast on me the imputation of malignity or cant. I regret but one thing in the course of these debates; I deeply regret that I should have been accused of calumniating

hole body of masters—I totally disclaim it—I should
hamed of myself if I held such language towards a
of men that can boast of as worthy and munificent
individuals as ever supported or adorned the institutions of
this country—nor am I, because I address myself to a particular evil, to be considered as the enemy of the Factory
System—remove some few imperfections, and it may
become a blessing, if not absolutely, at any rate relatively
to the present state of our labouring people.

Sir, when I first introduced this subject, I did not
attempt to handle the commercial argument—I did not think
it necessary for my view of the question, nor do I now; but
I owe it to those, whose interests I represent, to shew that
I have not left any part without due consideration; that I
have not rushed, like an enthusiast, into this career, neither
knowing nor caring what consequences might ensue from
the attainment of my ends. I said then, that I entertained
a full confidence that what was morally wrong could not be
politically right; I had, and I have, an equal confidence
that what is morally right cannot be politically wrong;
and every thing, that I can acquire by thinking, reading,
and, above all, by communication with those who are able
to instruct me from their practical experience, confirms my
conclusion.

And now, Sir, I shall entreat with much respect and
earnestness, the indulgence of the House to a subject,
always perhaps dry, and now both dry and somewhat exhausted.

Now, after all that has been written and said on the
subject, I can discover no more than four arguments
urged by our opponents against this measure, all of which
are comprised in the Manchester Petition lately presented
to this House

1st. That the passing of a ten hours' bill would cause a
diminution of produce

2nd. That there would take place a reduction, in the
same proportion, of the value of the fixed capital employed in the trade.

3rd. That a diminution of wages would ensue, to the
great injury of the workmen.

4th. A rise of price, and consequent peril of foreign
competition.

Even supposing that these assertions be separately, they

cannot be collectively, true; it is very fair to place before us a variety of possible contingencies, but it must not be urged that we are threatened by a combination of them. Any one event may occur; but such an occurrence prevents, in one case at least, the full accomplishment of the other.

Let us look at the first argument, that "the passing of a ten hours' bill would cause a diminution of produce."—It has hitherto been urged by all our antagonists that a reduction of one-sixth of the time would involve a corresponding reduction of one-sixth of the produce. I am happy to say that the opponents of the Bill have somewhat receded from their ground, and state, in their petition, an abatement of one-seventh; this is so far a gain on our side of the argument. But is the case so? What authority do they urge for the assertion? do they quote any facts? None on the face of the petition. But I think I shall be able to urge some very sufficient reasons to disprove altogether these general assertions, and establish some more favourable to myself.

The first statement to which I shall refer, is contained in a letter from a gentleman who carries on a very large concern; employing, I believe, no less than 1,200 hands; it is dated March, 1844.—" It is a mistaken notion," writes this gentleman, " to suppose that the produce of yarn or cloth from machinery, would be curtailed in an arithmetical proportion to the proposed reduction of working hours from twelve to ten, because in very many instances the workman can produce much or little during the day, as he feels disposed, or as his strength enables him; and in my own trade, in which we employ at least 1,200 hands, I have proved, beyond a doubt, that whenever we have reduced the hours for working from twelve to ten per day, which is equal to one-sixth, the quantity of work produced has not fallen below one-tenth or even one-twelfth." Another very important testimony is to be found in a valuable essay, published in 1831, entitled, " An Inquiry into the State of the Manufacturing Population," and written, I believe, by the owner of the largest establishment in Europe, Mr. Gregg:—" That a reduction of the hours of labour would cause a corresponding reduction in the quantity produced," says the writer, " we entirely deny; it is probable, that if factories were to work ten hours instead of twelve, the loss in the quantity produced would not be one sixth, but only about one-twelfth, and in mule spinning scarcely so much.

We know that in some cases, when the mills only worked four days in the week, they have often produced five days' quantity, and the men earned five days' wages. That this would be the case to a considerable extent every one must be aware, as all men will be able to work much harder for ten hours than they can for twelve."—Another gentleman who is the proprietor of a large establishment, writes to me thus:—" I am persuaded by experience, and from actual experiment, that the mill occupier would lose very littleby such a regulation (a ten hours' bill) : the workers would be so improved in their physical condition, that they would do very nearly as much work in ten and a half as in twelve hours."—Now, I have been anxious to obtain upon this point the opinion also of the operative cotton-spinners themselves, and I submitted two questions to them to which I have received answers from twenty of the principal towns in Lancashire. My first question was, " Is the reduction in the produce in the direct proportion of the reduction in time—that is, would a reduction of one-sixth in the hours of work lead to the reduction of one-sixth in the amount of produce ?" The answer I have received from twenty principal manufacturing towns was " Certainly not." My next question was, " At how much do you estimate the reduction of produce?" The answer took the view the most advantageous to my opponents, and was, " Not more than one-eighth."

So far, then, as argument can go, and practical opinion, the case is established ; there is no set-off to this statement; at least I have heard none ; our adversaries have no where adduced actual facts to shew that the abatement of produce is, in any degree, proportionate to the abatement of time.

Now the second argument may very probably follow on the foundation of the first, that " a reduction would take " place, in the same proportion, of the value of the fixed " capital employed in the trade ;"—this is not unlikely—but what does it amount to ? Great authorities have calculated the diminution of produce by one-twelfth or about 8 per cent. Let us admit this sum, as indicating the amount of the diminution of value on the fixed capital. Is this pure loss ? are there no compensating circumstances ? Look at this estimate furnished to me by one of the largest proprietors in the Cotton trade of England.—Here it is :

" Calculations of expenditure saved by diminution of hours of labour.—Horse power at work in the concern, 200 ; Original fixed capital, £100,000, or £500 per horse power, which is the usual estimate. Diminution of produce by reason of two hours less labour, I will say 10 per cent., putting the argument advantageously for my opponents, for the reduction of produce will not exceed 1-12th. The calculation will then stand thus :—On 12 hours time, or 69 hours per week, the quantity of production is now measured by 69 hours ; and this table will shew the yearly cost of fixed capital—

Interest on fixed capital at 5 per cent. per annum - - 5
Depreciation by wear and tear - - - - - - - 6
Coal, oil, tallow, repairs, &c. - - - - - - - - 12
Gas (nearly) - - - - - - - - - - - - 1

Total - - - - - - - 24

That is, 24 per cent. of the fixed capital for carrying on the concern, for a production of 69—say 69,000 bundles of manufactured goods—then 24 divided by 69=24·69, which is nearly ⅜ per cent. per annum of the fixed capital for each thousand bundles.

On 10 hours time, or 59 hours per week, the production being calculated at 10 per cent. less, may be measured by 62 hours production—

Interest on fixed capital at 5 per cent. per annum - - 5
Depreciation by wear and tear - - - - - - - 5
Coal, oil, tallow, repairs, &c. - - - - - - - 10
Gas (half). . - - - - - - - - - - - ½

Total - - - - - - 20½

That is 20½ per cent. of the fixed capital for carrying on the concern for the production of 62,000 bundles—then 20½ divided by 62=20½·62, which is a trifle less per 1,000 bundles than when working 12 hours, so far as the fixed capital is concerned. Now from the above table, it appears that the cost of goods (allowing the wages to be reduced in proportion to the work done) will be less than at present."

But the cardinal argument of my honourable opponents is hung on the supposed reduction of the operative's wages, and on the calculated mischiefs that would ensue to the work-people from so large an abatement of their weekly earnings. Sir, I have already observed, and I must observe again that these statements, founded, as they principally are on the researches of Mr. Horner, must be taken with many grains of allowance ; Mr. Horner, with perfect candour, admits the plea, when he tells us that he draws all his inferences from the statements by the masters, and that he has never been able to obtain, on the other side, the statements of the work-people. This is an important consideration; the men themselves take a different view; and while they admit an abatement of earnings, urge that it will be in a lower proportion. Sir, very hard things are said about the folly, and the nonsense, with other expressions equally pointed, of expecting twelve hours wages for ten hours work. Sir, I am not aware that anybody expected any such thing. It should be borne in mind that the earnings of these work-people are regulated by the piece, and not by time; that a man receives, every week, a certain sum, not for the labour, but for the produce of sixty-nine hours; and the abatement of his wages will be estimated, not by the limitation of the time, but by the reduced amount of yarn or cloth that he carries to the counting-house. A reduction of one-sixth of the time may involve, as I have endeavoured to shew, a reduction of one-twelfth of their earnings. Should the demand continue, and there is nothing in this bill to effect either the demand, or the rate of spinning per pound, the wages will fall only in proportion to the abatement of produce, one-tenth or one-twelfth, for the prices of labour will be governed, like those of all commodities, by the demand and supply.

To this extent the operatives anticipate fully a reduction of their earnings: I endeavoured to shew, some short time back, the calculations of household economy, by which they were prepared to meet even an abatement of one-sixth; —this, however, is beyond the mark—the countervailing advantages of a reduced time are so great, as compared with a reduction of wages, that they readily accept the loss, and find their interest in the improvement of health of body and mind; in social and domestic comfort; in the practice of household economy; and specially in the prolongation, by three or four years of their working life, of their physical capacities to obtain a livelihood.

The fourth and last argument with which I have to deal is founded on an apprehended rise of price, and consequent advantages to the foreign competitor. Now, on this head I must produce two calculations exhibiting very minutely the degree to which such a result may take place. I will state it as founded on two establishments. The amount of sunk capital in each is £20,000; each having 40-horse power at work, one spinning No. 36, the principal

count of yarn used ; the other manufacturing shirting cloth
from the same :—

SPINNING ESTABLISHMENT, WORKING 69 HOURS PER
WEEK, AND SPINNING 16,000lbs. OF NO. 36.

Weekly wages paid - - -	£87	10	0
wear and tear, coal, oil, gas expenses, carriage, &c. - - -	49	0	0
interest on capital sunk, at 5 per cent.	19	5	0
depreciation on capital, at 5 per cent.	19	5	0
profits at 10 per cent. per annum, on the capital - - -	38	10	0
	£213	10	0

WEAVING ESTABLISHMENT, WORKING 69 HOURS, AND
WEAVING 3,350 PIECES OF SHIRTINGS PER WEEK.

Weekly wages paid - - -	£233	6	8
wear and tear, oil, coal, gas expenses, carriage, &c. - - -	78	3	4
interest on capital sunk, at 5 per cent.	19	5	0
depreciation on capital at 5 per cent.	19	5	0
profits at 10 per cent. per annum, on the capital - - -	38	10	0
	£338	10	0

Again, the time being reduced to 60 hours, or one-seventh less,
as before observed, the production will not be reduced more
than one-eighth, that is to say :—

SPINNING ESTABLISHMENT, WORKING 60 HOURS PER WEEK,
WILL PRODUCE 14,000lbs. OF NO. 36 YARN.

Weekly wages paid - -	£76	10	0
wear and tear, coal, oil, gas, &c. expenses, carriage, &c. being 1-7th less - - - -	42	0	0
interest on capital sunk, at 5 per cent., as before - -	19	5	0
depreciation on capital, at 5 per cent., less 1-7th - -	16	10	0
profits, at 10 per cent., per annum, on capital, as before - -	38	10	0
	£192	15	0

This is the total cost for spinning 14,000lbs., allowing profits
and interest to remain the same, which is $3\frac{3}{10}d$ per lb., or
1-10th part of a penny more when working 60 hours instead
of 69.

WEAVING ESTABLISHMENT, WORKING 60 HOURS PER WEEK, WILL PRODUCE 2,950 PIECES OF SHIRTING.

Weekly wages paid - - -	£205	0	0
wear and tear, coal, oil, gas expenses, carriage, &c. 1-7th less - -	67	0	0
interest on capital sunk, at 5 per cent., as before - -	19	5	0
depreciation on capital, at 5 per cent., less 1-7th - -	16	10	0
profits at 10 per cent. per annum, on capital, as before - -	38	10	0
	£346	5	0

Which is the total cost for manufacturing 2,950 pieces of shirtings, being 2s. 4d. per piece, or $\frac{5}{8}$ths of a penny more when working 60 hours instead of 69, allowing profits and interest to remain the same.

This, then, on a minute and accurate calculation, is the fair estimate of the advantage, if advantage it can be called, which is offered to the foreigner as a set off to the great advantages to be bestowed on our own people !

But, Sir, I should like to try the question by the test of experience, and examine what has really been the effect upon production and upon the earnings of the workmen in all those cases where the hours of labour have been reduced. Forebodings were uttered of the most melancholy description—were they, any of them, fulfilled? This great question was agitated from 1815 to 1819. Several witnesses of experience and character maintained before Committees of the Lords and Commons in 1816, 1818, and 1819, the same propositions as those laid down in the Manchester Petition of the present year, that is to say, "the diminution of produce, the rise of price, the reduction of wages." Now observe; the hours of labour, before the restriction of 1820, ranged between thirteen and sixteen in the day. The Secretary to the Associated Mill Owners in 1819, gave in the following table, which falls short of the exact truth; but this is its result—

The total number of cotton mills was 325. Of these 5 worked 66 hours a week; 19 ditto, 68 to 68½ ; 38 ditto, 69, the present duration — in all 62. But the 263 which remained worked in a range from 70 to 93 hours a week. The population employed in the 62 mills was 7,486. But the population in the 263 mills was nearly 50,000. Here observe what a large proportion of the workers were occupied on the long periods of labour. Well, what was the result. In 1819 the act passed, to take effect from January 1, 1820, which reduced the hours in all the cotton factories to twelve actual working hours. It had been most boldly asserted that there would be a diminution of produce; but how was this confirmed? I will just compare the prophecy and the issue. In three years, from 1817 to 1819 inclusive, the cotton wool imported was 451,934,946 lbs. Now 1820 was the first year under restriction of labour to 12 from 14 and 15 hours a day; in three years, from 1821 to 1823 inclusive, the cotton wool imported was 466,776,751 lbs. The estimated weekly consumption in those years, before restriction, was, in 1817, 2,051,400 lbs.; 1818, 2,132,000 lbs.; and 1819, 2,116,809 lbs. In the three years after restriction the weekly consumption was, in 1821, 2,476,800 lbs.; 1822, 2,750,100 lbs.; and 1823, 3,025,000 lbs. You must observe, too, there was no falling off in aggregate production: for instance, the average quantity of cotton yarn retained for home consumption, and exported in each year, before restriction, from 1818 to 1820, both inclusive, was 134,420,757 lbs.; whilst in the three years, from 1821 to 1823, after restriction, the quantity was 140,142,224 lbs. The official value of cotton goods exported from Great Britain in two years, 1818 and 1819, before restriction, was £37,988,893. In the three years after restriction, from 1821 and 1822, the official value was £46,202,208. The official value of yarns for the two years exported before restriction, in 1818 and 1819, was £2,882,529. In the two years after restriction, 1821 and 1822, the value was £4,250,450. Look to the aggregate of goods for five years before and five years after restriction; from 1815 to 1819, both inclusive, the aggregate official value of goods exported was £95,787,626. From 1821 to 1825, the aggregate official value was £124,090,698. The statement of yarns, did I enter upon it, would be still more striking.

But now, with respect to the second apprehension, which lay in "the consequent advance of prices, and in the advantage to the foreigner," that argument has proved no more true as to the past than I believe it will as to the future. The declared value of the cotton goods exported in 1818 and 1819, together, was £29,032,412 before restriction. But the declared value of cotton goods exported in 1821 and 1822, together, was after restriction only £28,321,210, being an increase of twenty-one and a half per cent. in the quantity, and a decrease of two and a half per cent in the price. The same statement holds good in respect of the yarns exported. The declared value of yarns exported in 1818 and 1819 was £4,902,088. The declared value in 1821 and 1822 was £4,915,207, being an increase of forty-seven and a half per cent. in the quantity, as nearly as possible, at the same cost. The same might be seen on an aggregate of five years. The declared value of goods exported before restriction from 1815 to 1819, both included, was £75,445,940. The declared value from 1821 to 1825, after restriction, was £72,249,105. But let us consider still further the advantage given, as is said, to the foreigner, with respect to two countries from which the competition is the greatest. The import of cotton wool into France for consumption in 1820 was 20,203,000 kilogrammes, or, at 100 kilogrammes to 220½ lbs. 44,547,615lbs. The same in 1840 was 52,942,000 kilogrammes, or about 116,737, 110 lbs. being an increase of 162 per cent. The export of cotton twist and woven cottons from France in 1820 was 1,441,000 kilogrammes. The same in 1840, 4,446,000 kilogrammes, being an increase of 208½ per cent. The consumption of cotton in America in 1826 (I cannot obtain an earlier year), was 103,483 bales, or 38,392,193 lbs. The same in 1840, was 297,288 bales, or 110,293,848 lbs. being an increase of 187 per cent. The total value of manufactures exported from America in 1826, was 1,138,125 dollars, as stated in *Hunt's Merchant's Magazine*, published at New York. The total value in 1840 was 3,549,607 dollars, being an increase of 212 per cent.

The statements respecting the French trade I believe to be strictly accurate, they are taken from Mr. MacGregor's tables. But now turn to the British trade. The imports of cotton wool into Great Britain for consumption in 1820 was 152,829,633 lbs. The import of cotton wool in 1840 was 592,488,010 lbs., being an increase of 288 per cent. The total of manufactured cottons (twist and goods) exported from Great Britain in 1820, as by official value, was £22,531,079. The total value exported in 1840 was £73,124,730, being an increase per cent. of 225. Thus, while foreign countries increased 162 per cent, in the first case (France) and 187 per cent, in the second (America) on the amounts respectively of 44,547,615 lbs, and 110,293,848 lbs. the British trade increased 288 per cent. on the amount of nearly 153 millions. In support of my argument I quote Mr. M'Culloch. " It is ludicrous in-deed," says that able writer, " to suppose that a half peo-pled country like America, possessed of boundless tracts of unoccupied land of the highest degree of fertility, should be able successfully to contend in manufacturing industry with an old, settled, fully peopled, and very rich country like Great Britain." Mr. M'Culloch speaks like a man of sense.

Now, the third point of alarm which I wish to test by the experience of the past, is the question urged so strongly then, and with double vehemence now, the reduction of wages! Now, here is the actual statement of the case, which will shew how weak was the ground on which the assertion was based. I will take the facts without pretending to assign the causes. In 1818 and 1819, the two years preceding the limitation of the hours of labour, these were the wages of the operatives:—The fine spinners made £1. 12s per week, the coarse spinners from 20s to 28s per week, the women spinners 17s per week, the reelers 10s, the stretchers 14s, the pickers 9s. I find from the same table—a table in Tooke's " High and Low Prices"—that in 1820, the first year of the limitation, the wages continued the same. I have not been able to get any tables to shew the state of their earnings in the two following years; but the subject is a very important one, and we can arrive at it by an easy process. The records of the operative spinners in Lan-cashire shew for many years the prices paid for spinning per lb. In 1818 and 1819, in the Manchester and Bolton district, those prices were for 40s., $3\frac{1}{2}d$ per lb. ; 60s, $5\frac{1}{2}d$ lb. ; 80s, $8\frac{1}{4}d$ per lb.; 100s, 9d per lb. ; 150s, 1s 10d, per lb.; and 200s, 5s 4d per lb. I find that, in 1821 and 1822, the years following the limitation of labour, the same prices were obtained for spinning as in 1818 and 1819. I have already shewn to the House that the weekly consump-tion of cotton-wool, in the three years following the re-striction was greater than in the three years preceding the restriction. Therefore, as there was a greater quantity of cotton wool to be worked up, and the prices of working it up were not reduced, we have good ground for asserting that wages continued, at least, at the same level. So much for the predictions of wages to be reduced.

Did the loss then fall on the profit of the manufacturer ?
Suppose, for the sake of argument, that it was so; surely
an adequate return must have been left, for I find that the

Cotton wool imported in 1818, amounted to 177,282,158lbs.
But in 1842 to   .   .   475,060,700lbs.
The total number of cotton establishments in 1819 . 344
The same by latest returns (1839) .   .   1,815

And mills are, at this moment, in course of construction
in every quarter. But let people say what they will, the
whole subject is contained in an extract from a letter written
to me in March, 1844, by a very large proprietor :—

"When," says he, "we see around us men of all trades and
professions going into the cotton trade, some with little capital,
others with less knowledge or experience of the business—when
we see gentlemen, brokers, merchants, doctors, lawyers, drapers,
tailors, &c., leaving their respective professions and trades, and
see them building mills in almost every town in Lancashire—
when we see capital thus finding its way into the spinning and
manufacturing business, surely the profits cannot be so small that
a little reduction of the hours of labour to suffering thousands is
impracticable."

Now, Sir, I have long been regarded as a monomaniac
on these subjects, as a man of peculiar opinions, one having
a fixed idea, but without support, or even countenance, in
my wild opinions—yet is it not the fact that the reduction
of the hours of labour is a question maintained and desired
by many great manufacturers in the cotton-trade ? I may
quote in this House the Members for Oldham, Salford,
Ashton, and Blackburn—I will just indicate a few without
its walls, firm friends of the measure ; Mr. Kay, of Bury ;
Mr. William Walker, of Bury, perhaps the largest consumer
of cotton in that district ; Mr. Hamer, of the same place,
a partner in the firm of the late Sir Robert Peel; Mr.
Cooper, of Preston; Mr. Tysoe, of Salford ; and Mr. Ken-
worthy, of Blackburn. I set great store by the opinions
of this gentleman last named, because he has passed through
all the gradations of the business, and has by his own talent
and integrity, raised himself from the condition of an
operative to the station of a master. I may add, too, the
name of Mr. Hargreaves, of Accrington, no inconsiderable
person in Lancashire, who feels so strongly on this subject,
that he attended a public meeting in support of the question, and moved a resolution himself.

Now, consider here the famous argument of Mr. Senior, an argument urged almost more frequently than any other, to prove the folly and mischief of my demand. Every one, no doubt, will readily acknowledge the talents and learning of this gentleman, but practical experiments are worth ten thousand of his calculations. Mr. Senior declares that the profit of the manufacturer arises from the labour of the last two hours ! Now observe—this assertion might be met in various ways by reasoning, but a fact is far better. I find a letter addressed, in April 1844, to the Editor of the " *Bolton Free Press*," and signed, a Bolton Cotton Spinner, but known to be by Mr. Thomason, a highly respectable mill-owner,—he speaks from personal experience ; and what does he say ? These are his words:—" There is also " another consideration for employers, namely, that in a " day's work of twelve hours, the last hour, by reason of the " exhaustion and listlessness of the workers, more especially " young children of thirteen or sixteen, is the least produc- " tive in quantity, and the least satisfactory in quality." And he adds, now mark this,—" The probability is, that " the twelfth hour produces more spoiled work than any " other two hours of the day." Here is the opinion of a practical cotton spinner ; and it is confirmed by every statement that I have received on the subject; not a few experienced persons having declared that they could tell, by the feel and the appearance of the cloth, whether it had been made at the earlier or later periods of the day. But, further, I submitted the question to the operative-spinners of Lancashire, and this is the answer I received from twenty principal towns:—" What is the character of the " work of the two last hours, is it equal in quality to that of " the first ?" The answer which they have given me is,—" Certainly not, especially in the winter months."

Sir, is it necessary further to detain the House by proofs, that the arguments of Mr. Senior rest, by no means, on the firmest grounds? The commercial argument, in truth, is really feeble; it has always been urged, and has never been verified, and yet experience should go for something in these great considerations,—it was broached in 1816; repeated and enforced in evidence before committees, in speeches and pamphlets, in 1817, 1818, and 1819, and utterly refuted by the whole subsequent history of the cotton trade from that day to the present—you had no diminution

of produce, no fall in wages, no rise in price, no closing of
markets, no irresistible rivalry from foreign competition,
although you reduced your hours of working from 16, 14,
13, to 12 hours in the day. What change has there occurred so mighty as to prevent a similar result in 1845? Is
British energy so exhausted, our skill so decayed, our resources so dried up, that two hours taken from 12 will produce nothing but misery, when 2, 3, or 4, taken from 16,
14, or 13, produced nothing but good? You argue, moreover, as though there existed no difference of opinion among
master cotton-spinners—as though every commercial authority lay on your side, and were not found in equal
weight and character upon ours.

But while your financial argument has failed, not so that
arising from moral considerations. The antagonists, even,
of the restriction pronounce it desirable, could it be safely
effected; and your own inspectors have told you, that without such a limitation of the hours of toil, there can be no
hopes for the social or moral improvement of the working
classes. Here, then, springs up a curious and important
problem for solution by this House—no, not by this House,
for they have already resolved it—but for her Majesty's
Government, who deny our conclusions, and oppose themselves to the thrice recorded wishes of the British empire.—
Which is the preferable condition for a people—high wages,
with privation of social and domestic enjoyment, without
the means of knowledge or the opportunities of virtue,
acquiring wages which they waste through ignorance of
household economy, and placed in a state of moral and
physical deterioration? or lower earnings, with increased
advantages for mental improvement and bodily health; for
the understanding and performance of those duties, which
now they either know not, or neglect; for obtaining the
humble, but necessary accomplishments of domestic life,
and cultivating its best affections? Clouds of witnesses
attest these things; clergy, ministers of every persuasion,
doctors, master-manufacturers, and operatives, have given,
and are ready to give again, the most conclusive evidence;
but her Majesty's Ministers refuse to listen, and will neither
adopt the remedy we propose, nor assist us with one of
their own.

Sir, this House is now placed in a novel position; it is
summoned to rescind its resolution, not because new facts

or new conditions have appeared, but because the Minister has declared his hostility. Nothing has been stated that was not stated before—no fresh knowledge communicated, no unseen dangers discovered. The house is summoned to cancel its vote, not upon conviction, but to save a government. The minister surely has no right to expose his supporters to this alternative — either to abandon their opinions or dislodge their political friends. A determination such as this should have been signified beforehand, and not reserved until a time when it will be obeyed certainly with great pain, and perhaps not without disgrace. Sir, I do think that members should pause to consider the precedent they are about to establish. Very alarming words fell from my honourable friend the member for Somersetshire—manly and conscientious as is everything that he says or does—that while he retained his opinions, he should change his conduct, because he found himself at variance with the Minister. And so it is come to this, that great questions are to be tried, not by their merits, but by their aspect as affecting the will or the fancies of a government, opposing, be it remembered, not a set of principles to introduce a new system of rule or policy, but asserting a mere opinion against the extension of an existing law, hastily taken up, and somewhat arbitrarily maintained. Sir, the whole question of representative governments is at stake—votes have been rescinded before, but never such as this ; you are almost declaring, to those who are your ordinary friends, that they shall never exercise a vote but at the will of the Minister. This is a despotism under the forms of the constitution ; and all to no purpose ; for your resistance will be eventually and speedily overcome, but your precedent will remain, more fatal to true liberty and independence than all the Reform Bills.

Sir, it is possible, nay more, it is probable (for their efforts have been great) that her Majesty's Ministers will carry the day; but for how long ?—If they would render their victory a lasting one, they must extinguish all the sentiments that gave rise to mine. Their error is stupendous—" Scilicet illo igne, vocem populi, et libertatem senatûs, et conscientiam humani generis aboleri arbitrabantur." Could you, simultaneously with your extinction of myself, extinguish for a while the sense of suffering, or at least all sympathy with it, you might indeed hope for an inglorious repose; and, by the indulgence of your own ease, heap up, for your posterity, turmoil, anxiety, and woe. But things will not end here. The question extends with numbers, strengthens with their strength, and rises with their intelligence. The feeling of the country is roused; and, so long as there shall be voices to complain and hearts to sympathise, you will have neither honour abroad, nor peace at home, neither comfort for the present, nor security for the future.—But I dare to hope for far better things—for restored affections, for renewed understanding between master and man, for combined and general efforts, for large and mutual concessions of all classes of the wealthy for the benefit of the common welfare, and specially of the labouring people.—Sir, it may not be given to me to pass over this Jordan; other and better men have preceded me, and I entered into their labours; other and better men will follow me, and enter into mine; but this consolation I shall ever continue to enjoy—that, amidst much injustice, and somewhat of calumny, we have at last "lighted such a candle in England as, by God's blessing, "shall never be put out."

FACTORY LEGISLATION.

REPORT

OF

THE CENTRAL COMMITTEE

OF

THE ASSOCIATION OF MILL OWNERS

AND MANUFACTURERS,

ENGAGED IN THE COTTON TRADE,

FOR THE YEAR 1844,

AS ALSO UPON

THE RECENT PROCEEDINGS IN PARLIAMENT,

On the passing of the Factories Act.

AGREED UPON AT A MEETING HELD IN MANCHESTER, DEC. 31ST, 1844.

MANCHESTER:

PRINTED BY A. BURGESS & CO. 27, VICTORIA-STREET.

1845.

REPORT.

It will be borne in mind, by those connected with the Cotton Manufacture of this district, that early in the Parliamentary Session of 1844, a Factory Bill was introduced by Sir James Graham, containing provisions of so stringent a character as to be deemed wholly unrequired by any existing abuses.

That the members of this Association were, upon several very urgent occasions, called together to deliberate upon the Bill; that they considered its character altogether objectionable and offensive, and that having agreed upon numerous alterations and suggestions, they appointed a Deputation to submit them to Government, and to urge their adoption.

The Deputation had several interviews with Sir James Graham on the subject, in which they endeavoured to impress upon him that the Bill was utterly uncalled for, if not impracticable.

In the progress of the Bill through the House of Commons, a sudden and unlooked-for emergency arose, and the Home Secretary was pleased to avail himself of the timely assistance and practical information which the Deputation were enabled to supply.

This emergency arose out of an Amendment, proposed by Lord Ashley, to reduce the time of work in Mills, to *ten hours a day*. The Amendment was carried, and the Ministry defeated, although, singularly enough, in a subsequent stage of the proceedings, when the Ministry staked its existence on retaining the clause for twelve hours, the House was induced to reverse its own decision.

The Committee have satisfaction in believing, that, at this important juncture, the Deputation were enabled to afford important aid in preventing the threatened reduction of two hours a day from being imposed upon the trade; but they have to regret that in other respects their mission was attended with very little success.

It was a leading object with the Deputation to induce Government to omit altogether, or greatly to modify, those clauses which related to accidents, as well as other very objectionable

provisions in the Bill, on the ground that they were unprecedented, grievous in their operation, and utterly uncalled for
but, notwithstanding the array of facts adduced by the Deputation, it appeared obvious that Government were determined to
carry their own Bill, because, as was alleged, the necessity of
the measure was so strongly insisted upon by the Inspectors.

The Bill, with some slight modification, has become the law
of the land, and is now being enforced with rigid strictness; but,
since its general and stringent application is considered by many
persons to be impracticable, the period of its existence may
possibly be very limited, and its failure may again lead to farther
interference.

Under these circumstances it becomes the duty of the Manufacturers to consider their true position in the country, and
the evils to which they are constantly exposed by legislative
intermeddling.

It is believed that no Manufacturer can have forgotten the
many years of abusive agitation through which himself and
his brethren have passed, nor the harassing perplexities to
which his trade has been constantly subjected:—nor do the
Committee see any reason to expect that these annoyances are
about to subside, but on the contrary, judging from the menac-
ing attitude of the parties usually concerned, it is evident that
the agitation is intended to be kept up.

By the following letter from Lord Ashley to Mr. Henry Green,
the Secretary of the Manchester Short Time Committee, it
would appear that future proceedings on this momentous question are to be anticipated:—

"London, Nov. 27, 1844.
"SIR,—In answer to your letter, in which you desire, on the part of the
Operatives of Lancashire, to learn what course I shall think advisable, in the
ensuing session of parliament, I must reply that I see no reason why the question
of the ten hours' bill should not be renewed at the earliest possible period. I will
endeavour, on the first night of our meeting, to fix a day for bringing the subject
again under the consideration of the house.—I am, sir, your very obedient servant,

"Mr. Henry Green, Secretary."   "ASHLEY."

The Committee therefore feel strongly impressed, that it is the
duty of Manufacturers, as a body, to sustain the right estimation
of the class to which they belong, and to determine in what
manner they shall deal with the slander and falsehood which,
under pretence of the agitation of this question, is continually
poured upon them. They would also draw attention to the
necessity of considering by what means the character of the
Trade shall hereafter be defended, and its true interests maintained.

The Committee have already devoted some attention to this subject, and passing over the minor slanderers who have been employed to promulgate falsehood, they would refer to some of the absurd mis-statements appearing in the speeches of Lord Ashley, during the last Session, and which, it is believed, induced many Members of Parliament (relying upon such high authority) to support his Lordship's views.

LORD ASHLEY'S MIS-STATEMENTS.

It may surprise many of those who are conversant with the habits and practical details of the Cotton Manufacture to be informed, that in one of the speeches of Lord Ashley, as reported in the " Morning Post," the following most extraordinary allegations appear. Lord Ashley declared that he was prepared to prove, that "since the year 1815, those engaged in Mill labour " endured a three-fold amount of toil to what they did then," and "that spinners in their movements had to travel as follows :

In 1815, Eight miles per day.
1832, Twenty miles do.
1839, lowest distance, fifteen miles do.
1839, highest do. thirty-seven miles do.

That "the mere travelling" was not "the whole labour of the " piecers and spinners, they had many other laborious occupa- " tions besides following the locomotion.

" That in 1815 the spinners put up 820 stretches per day on " each pair of mules.

| 1832 | ,, | 2200 | ,, |
| 1844 | ,, | 2400 | ,, |

" That the calculations of distances gone over had been made " for him (Lord Ashley), at his request, by one of the *most* " *experienced Mathematicians* in the Country—"that he had made " these measurements and calculations on the spot"—and in five " different mills, spinning respectively Nos. 14, 15, 30, 38, and " 40's yarn.

That in addition to the labour of travelling, there was also " the strain of leaning over the machinery, and bringing the body " again to an upright position"—" the fatigue of turning the body " round and reversing its direction not less than from 4,000 to " 5,000 times a day."

Referring to Mr. Greg's statement of the distances travelled in 1836 (about eight miles a day), Lord Ashley stated that he had referred it to the *Mathematician* before alluded to,

who had reported to him "that Mr. Greg's statement must
" either be the result of some *strange* and *grievous blundering,*
" or a *gross perversion* of. *observed facts.*"

Lord Ashley further stated that "in the *card room* one person
" now did the work of two, and that without any increased
" wages." In the weaving room a person had written to him
that "there had been an increase of at least 10 per cent of
" labour, during the last four years."

" In power-loom weaving the number of picks in
1819, were 60 per minute.
1842, ,, 104 ,,
" Such an amount of toil as this, carried on in close and ill-
" ventilated rooms, where many noxious exhalations prevailed,
" must cause the most serious physical evils to the human frame
" and constitution."

" That he," Lord Ashley, "when in Lancashire, visited the
" Mills, and Infirmaries, and was surprised to find the wards
" filled with scrofulous cases, all of which were Factory cases."

" That Dr. Villermé, who had been commissioned by the French
" Government to enquire into the factory system in France and
" Belgium, reported the tendency of the employment to produce
" coughs and pulmonary complaints, and early death. "

Lord Ashley also stated that factory employment injured the
eyes, and caused "lamentable accidents, of which the House had
" now records, and even these minor accidents, as they were
" called,—the loss of fingers and hands—almost all occurred
" during the last hour of the evening, when the people were so
" blind, tired, and sleepy, that they almost became reckless of
" danger."

" That the age of forty was an age *rarely* to be found amongst
" those employed in a Cotton Mill," and that " the miserable oc-
" cupants of human frames"—'cast-off *Factory hands*' — were
maintained by their children, or were sweeping streets, gather-
ing rags, selling salt, picking up dung, begging, or engaged in
employments of a similar character.

" That the tendency of improvements in machinery," says
Inspector Horner (1835), "is more and more to substitute *infant*
" for *adult* labour," and that he was informed that in some
establishments the preference is given to females, more especially
to those who have *families* at home dependent on them for
support.

That unmarried females working in Mills, are ignorant of
any domestic duties; and the married, untidy, dirty, slovenly,
cannot sew, take care of children, cannot manage the house
expenses, are guilty of perpetual waste and extravagance—

leaving their children to the care of ill-paid and unsuitable persons, and having recourse to ' Godfrey's Cordial,' 'to lull their troubles.'

That one of the evil consequences entailed by the substitution of female labour was "the total disruption of domestic life," the men looking after household affairs, or rambling about the streets, unemployed, whilst the burden of maintaining the family has rested almost exclusively on the wife and children. " That women, while performing the labour of men, were adopting men's habits and amusements "—" meeting together in " clubs, to drink, sing, and smoke"—and using "the lowest, most " brutal, and most disgusting language." In illustration of this Lord Ashley related to the house a disgusting pot-house dialogue in which the husband was represented as very pathetically intreating his drunken wife to return to her " crying bairn," and the wife offering liquor to her husband, but refusing to return to her child, and reproaching him as " an idle devil."

Lord Ashley declined, or did not deem it necessary, to satisfy the house upon the *commercial* view of the question ; and to consider the safety of diminishing, by *one-sixth*, the manufacturing power of the country, and, as an inevitable consequence of effecting a reduction of wages to a much greater extent.

REFUTATION OF MIS-STATEMENTS.

It was not to be wondered, that such slanderous mis-statements should create a strong sense of indignation throughout the trade, nor that they should occasion that extraordinary excitement which prevailed in the House of Commons on the question. The Committee of the Association of Millowners did not fail to remark these effects, and they immediately proceeded to endeavour to disabuse the public mind, by the diffusion, in a statistical form, of such authentic information as they deemed calculated to refute the extraordinary allegations of Lord Ashley, and suitable for the guidance of Members of the House of Commons, in considering the provisions of the bill.

This information was procured during the Easter recess, by the issuing of circulars to all the manufacturing firms whose names appeared in the Directory, and the Committee have to acknowledge the great promptitude with which such information was supplied.

Meanwhile the Deputation in London perceiving that some considerable time must necessarily elapse before this information

could be obtained, and fearing that the unchecked circulation
of so much falsehood, given upon high authority, was calculated
to bring unmerited obloquy upon the general body of Manufacturers, at once issued a Memorial signed by Mr. Henry Ashworth,
and addressed to the Members of the House of Commons, cau-
tioning and requesting them carefully to examine the evidence
as to the alleged facts, by which an interference with the hours
of labour was sought to be justified, and appealing to the well-
known and devoted anxiety of a large number of the Master
Manufacturers to advance the social condition and promote the
comforts of the operatives.

The deputation undertook to assert upon their own authority,
aided by information promptly furnished by Messrs. Horrocks,
Miller & Co., Messrs. Paul Catterall Son, & Co., and Mr Wm.
Taylor, of Preston, that with some few exceptions, the distance
traversed by spinners and piecers was *under* 8 *miles a day*, and
not as had been stated by Lord Ashley, varying from 15 *to* 37
Miles per day.

The Deputation also drew attention, to the unfair manner, in
which Lord Ashley had quoted the authority of Dr. Villermé, to
prove the tendency of the Cotton Manufacture " *to produce
coughs, pulmonary consumptions, and early death,* " and shewed
from Dr. Villermé's own words, that so far from making this statement, or anything like it, that he had rather asserted the direct
contrary.

That Dr. Villermé, did indeed attribute such a tendency to one
branch of the Manufacture, as practised in France, viz. the process of " batting cotton," a process disused in England for more
than 20 years, but he stated that wherever he found that *batting*
had been superseded by Machinery, the evil was almost entirely
obviated.

The Deputation also remarked upon Lord Ashley's uncandid
omissions in his quotations from Dr. Villermé; they shewed that
Dr. Villermé stated—" That, with the exceptions of the process
of ' Batting ' and to some extent that of Carding, the condition
of nearly all the persons engaged in the Cotton Manufacture
of France, is superior to the Operatives who work in their own
houses, adding, very quaintly, that "Men may ask Government
" to prevent all evils, just as they would ask Physicians to cure all
" diseases; but no amelioration of the operative's condition will
" follow ; it is not quite so easy to do good in this world, as some
" people imagine it to be."

In the course of a week, or ten days, from the issuing of the
circulars to the manufacturing firms, the Committee received
returns from 474 master manufacturers, and immediately pro-

ceeded to draw up an analysis of the information so obtained, which was placed in the hands of Members of Parliament as a "STATEMENT OF FACTS."

Petitions embodying the information contained in these returns were also addressed to both houses of Parliament. Such returns proved that the average distance travelled by each piecer, was *under 8½ miles a day,* fully corroborating the statement previously signed by Mr. Henry Ashworth, and exceeding only by a fraction of a mile the calculation which Mr. R. H. Greg had 8 years before made, and published, and the accuracy of whose statements Lord Ashley had impeached.

The Returns also shewed that there was no foundation whatever for the assertion, " That improvements in Machinery had led to the substitution of infant for adult labour, or to the increase of female, as compared with male employment." On the contrary, they proved " that the proportion of *Children under* 13 *years of age,* to the total number of Factory Operatives, employed was as follows:—

	In 1835.	1844.
Children under 13...	13 per cent.	3½ per cent.
Females	54 ,,	52½ ,,
Adult Males	26½ ,,	32 ,,

Thus did the Returns of the Mill Owners prove *the very reverse of the statements put forth by Lord Ashley.*

Minute particulars were also obtained as to the employment of the Husband of every married female working in these Mills, and it appeared that only *one in twelve of the husbands of the females at work was unemployed.*

The Association after due enquiries ascertained that there was just as little ground for the assertion "That persons of 40 years and upwards were usually discharged, as unfit for factory employment."

It was proved that, whilst females usually quitted work in the factories soon after marriage, or the birth of the first or second child, men continue their labour in factories, in as large a proportion as in other equally well paid employments ; the Returns showing that the number at work of 40 years old and upwards, *is* 60 *per cent of the total proportion of males living between the ages of* 40 *and* 60, taking the number of males employed between 21 and 40 as the standard of comparison.

It was most gratifying to the committee to perceive by the returns, that the number of accidents in Mills was so very small. They considered this a most important part of the information obtained, since from the provisions of the Bill in relation to accidents, the world at large might be led to infer that they were of constant occurrence.

Out of 412 Mill Owners making returns, 167 reported the following accidents as having occurred within an average period of 20½ years, viz; 72 occasioning death, 168 loss of limb, and 13 not specified. 196 Mill Owners reported that no accident involving loss of life, or limb, had occurred in their factories in an average period of 13½ years.

The proportion of accidents, therefore, appears to have been about *one death per annum in* 104 *Mills, and one loss of limb in* 41 *Mills.* From 49 of the Mills no returns were made with respect to accidents.

It appeared that 412 Mills employed 116,281 persons, being an average of 282 in each Mill ; therefore, *in* 104 *Mills employing* 29,328 *persons, only one fatal accident in a year occurs ;* and *in* 41 *Mills employing* 11,562 *persons, only one accident occasioning loss of limb* occurs in the same period. The Committee venture to assert that so favorable a result as to accidents probably cannot be obtained from any other industrial occupation in this country.

From the Return by the Coroners in the Factory Districts it appeared that out of upwards of 858 accidents, occasioning loss of life, *only* 29 (3 2-5*ths per cent*) *have been occasioned by Factory Machinery,* while 79 have been caused by Carts &c. and 85 occurred in Coal Pits.

The Returns further shewed that no less than 82 per cent of the whole number of Factory Operatives can read, while it appears from the Registrar's Returns for England, that about one half of the whole population of the country do not know how to write their names.

Some of the Mill Owners neglected to make a return of the amount of wages paid by them ; but returns were made by Mill Owners employing 112,796 operatives, and the total amount of net weekly wages paid by them was, £57,881 18s. 1d. ; *or an average weekly wages to each operative of* 10s. 3½d. *net,* being a reduction of 2d. per week in the average wages of each operative since 1833, as shewn by a similar statement then published, of 151 Mills employing 48,645 persons. It is well known that since the period of these returns, a general rise, varying from 5 to 10 per cent, has taken place in every branch of the trade.*

* Some of the allegations made by Lord Ashley, the Committee did not consider of sufficient moment to advert to,—such for instance as the prevalence of Scrofula— a complaint, for which the mothers of children so affected, have, it is well known, considered mills, from their warm and equal temperature, as curative.

Mr. Daniel Noble, Surgeon, of Manchester, who undertook at the instance of Dr. Forbes, the learned Editor of the " British and Foreign Medical Review," " Special Researches on the influence of Manufactures upon Health," says, " I wish " by no means to constitute myself the apologist of the Factory System, as it stands. " * * * * Assuredly it ought not to be deemed curative of or protective

In all the Manufacturing districts there are several trades such as those of Colliers, Engineers, Ironfounders, Machine Makers, Builders, Tailors, Shoemakers, &c. which do not employ *female labour*; and to the wives and daughters of the persons engaged, in such trades, the Spinning and Weaving Mills afford the means of contributing by their labour, to the support of their families. From enquiries made in Bolton, in 1836, it was found that there were more than 3000 operatives engaged in those trades, from which *women were excluded*, and consequently a very large number of families would have been stinted, if not deprived of some of the necessaries of life, had the resources which they derived from the labour of their female relatives been interrupted. It is perfectly well known that when employment for females cannot be obtained in Mills, it is sought for in other branches of industry, involving occupations far more injurious to health, and dangerous to morals, than those of mills, and cotton factories. This is felt by the females themselves; they prefer Mills to most other occupations, and even *to domestic service.*

The smallness of the number of persons above 40 years of age, engaged in Mills, does not arise so much from superannuation, as from the number of mill hands, who are enabled by their savings to enter into superior occupations. No fewer than 197 persons who had quitted Factories were traced in the town and vicinity of Ashton-under-lyne, notwithstanding the short space of time allowed and the obvious delicacy and difficulty of such inquiries. Of these 197 it was found that 14 had become Master Spinners and Manufacturers, 61 Shopkeepers, 42 Publicans and Beer Retailers, 11 Grocers and Tea Dealers, and the rest had formed other respectable means of obtaining a livelihood. The Committee would venture to submit that there are very few industrial occupations which would afford similar evidence of advancement in a single locality.

It may indeed be true as stated, that in the year 1841 several distressed Spinners were found in mean and degrading occupations; but it must be remembered that the greater part of that year was a season of extraordinary depression when many mills were standing, and others were working short time. But even if the returns of distress were perfectly accurate, they would only prove

" from scrofulous disease, as some would appear to maintain.   *   *   *

After shewing in detail that the Factory System is not the cause of premature puberty, of scrofula, or of consumption, Mr. Noble concludes as follows :—

" In bringing this treatise to a close I think myself in some degree entitled, from " all that has preceded, to conclude that *no peculiar evils attach necessarily to* " *Manufacturing pursuits.*"   *   *   *   " I think however that upon a " review of the facts and circumstances discussed in the preceding pages, the evils " afflicting the working classes, in this point of view will be considered to appertain " to their *domestic* rather than their *industrial* relations."

that a compulsory working of short time, which depressed markets can enforce more strongly than any Legislative enactment, deteriorates the condition of the Operative and subjects him to want and degradation.

The slanderous imputation upon factory employment "that it "has a tendency to unfit females for the duties of domestic life, "and to reverse the condition of the sexes," carrying upon the face of it so much the appearance of inconsiderate rashness, and, like the other allegations of Lord Ashley, given upon anonymous authority, the Committee did not consider deserving of serious refutation.

In the "Address" and "Statement of Facts" which the Committee thought proper to issue to Members of Parliament and others, they stated that the information they conveyed was based upon returns sent in by gentlemen of character and established reputation, and that the parties whose names were attached were not only willing, but anxious to afford every opportunity of scrutinizing the accuracy of those returns.

The Committee cannot but regret that a measure so seriously affecting the interests of themselves and the operatives should have been dealt with by the Legislature in a manner so hasty, amidst so many obvious exaggerations and mis-statements put forth upon anonymous, or questionable authority.

During the debates on the Factory Bill the attention of Parliament was drawn *to the class of persons who usually furnish to Members of Parliament information respecting factories*, who frequent the lobbies of the House, and who appear in London under the title of "*Deputies from the Operatives.*"

It was openly stated in the House of Commons of one of these deputies, — who had published two books dedicated to Lord Ashley, exposing what he called the Factory System, and who had been paraded before visitors in Lord Ashley's house as a "*Factory Cripple*", — that whilst collecting the materials of one of these books he had been furnished with money by Lord Ashley, that he had received written instructions from an individual, who it was admitted acted as Lord Ashley's agent, to "blacken the characters" of certain Mill Owners who took a prominent part in opposing the Ten Hours' Bill—and that he had lately been discarded by Lord Ashley, who stated in the House of Commons that he had discovered him to be a man unworthy of credit.

It was also stated of another of these "Operatives" and Delegates that he had first obtained employment in a mill in Manchester by means of a forged certificate of character, dated Belfast, and that he had since been twice in prison. And, of

another "Operative" and frequenter of the lobby of the House
of Commons, a newspaper report was read shewing that he had
recently been arrested, and had taken his trial upon a charge
of stealing silver plate from a tavern.

It was strongly urged by the Association, and by the Deputation in London, that whilst the evils of the Factory System,
especially with regard to the operatives, have been most grossly
exaggerated, the advantages, both as regards steadiness of
employment and amount of remuneration have been generally
overlooked, and the Committee did not hesitate to repudiate
the charge that factory labour is more severe or less healthy
than that of other employments.

It is useless to discuss whether the present arrangement of
twelve hours a day for five days, and nine hours on Saturdays,
is precisely the best limitation for labour. It is the limitation
which Parliament has long since established, and by which it
has deemed it right to abide throughout the numerous attempts
to shew that the time was excessive. Usage and habit have
accommodated themselves to this period; the expenditure of
concerns, the rates of wages, and of exchanges with other men's
labour, have become regulated and adjusted by it;—moreover,
upon the continued assurance of this limitation, the Master
Manufacturer has based his calculations of a profitable return,
and on the faith of its existence has embarked his capital.
Indeed so much importance has been attached to this limitation
that, upon a recent attempt to disturb it, a powerful Ministry
placed itself in the gap, and, as before stated, staked its existence upon the measure.

In conclusion, the Committee have to observe, and they cannot
withdraw their attention from the fact, that in this Country the
hours of labour in Mills have already been reduced below those of
any other Country.* That under this disadvantage the British
Manufacturer has hitherto been enabled to combat foreign rivalry
chiefly by the superiority of his Machinery, secured to him by an
exclusive privilege which prevented its exportation. Latterly

* In the debates on the Factory Bill, Sir R. Peel stated on the authority of
M. Ducpetiaux, a member of the Belgian Government Commission, that the number
of hours, which Mills run in the principal Manufacturing Countries, was as follows.

United States	78 hours per week.
France	72 to 84 ,,
Prussia	72 to 90 ,,
Switzerland	78 to 84 ,,
Austria	72 to 80 ,,
Saxony	72 ,,
Baden	84 ,,
Bonn	94 ,,
England	69 ,,

by an Act allowing the free exportation of Machinery, this compensating advantage has been withdrawn. The British Manufacturer has now no advantage over the foreigner, excepting in the experience and training of his hands, and the facilities of internal traffic ; whilst he has to contend against foreign establishments having the best British machinery, longer hours of labour, abundance of water power, greater cheapness in food productions, and a lower rate of wages.

The Manufacturers of this country as a body have never resisted the exportation of Machinery, and the Committee repudiate the idea that they desire to possess any privilege or exclusive advantage over the foreign Manufacturer. They have already alluded to the relative position of both, and submit to the British people whether it would not appear like hard dealing if our Legislature, after this surrender of British skill to foreign rivalry, should increase the boon by a further curtailment of our manufacturing labour.

The importance of resisting the reduction of labour in Mills, the Committee considered paramount, believing, as they do, that under existing circumstances, the passing of a " Ten Hours Bill," might be termed an "Act to export British Capital;" and that in reference to British enterprise, it would be taken as "notice to quit."

There can be no doubt, that even with an abridgement of the hours of labour, some portion of the trade would still remain in this country ; but that which remained would be a withered branch, it would cease to afford to the multitudes of our workpeople the amount of wages and command of comforts which, happily, they now enjoy, and possibly would bring upon them an inconceivable extent of destitution and misery.

Therefore, on behalf of our common country, which has derived, and is now continuing to derive, so large a portion of its resources from the productive power of its manufacturing industry :—on behalf of the manufacturing capitalist, the merchant, and the thousands of other tradesmen, as well as that very numerous body of professional men who are also equally dependant upon the existence of our manufactures, and who together may be said to constitute the middle class and moral strength of our country ; and on *behalf of the working classes* themselves, it necessarily behoves not only the Association of Master Manufacturers, but also every firm friend of humanity and justice, to unite in their endeavours to avert impending evils, from whatsoever quarter, or in whatsoever garb they may appear.

The Committee are aware that with no inconsiderable number of Master Manufacturers, an impression has prevailed, that the calumnious mis-statements of our opponents were undeserving of notice, or refutation. We know that there are many persons who deem it a pardonable error to disregard slander, and who content themselves with the confiding assurance, that, notwith-standing what others may say to vilify them, it will still remain an undeniable truth, that they, as Manufacturers, individually and collectively, have bettered their country; but we intreat them to consider whether by indulging in a disregard of the slanderous imputations of their opponents, they are not forgetful of their own self-respect, and neglectful of a duty to the order to which they belong.

It is very possible that no attack upon Factory labour may be seriously meditated; and even if the threatened attack were to be made, there is the possibility that its leaders may not again consider the use of slander and *exaggeration* as the best means to effect their object. Nevertheless, there can be no doubt that occasions will arise, in which a large amount of valuable information, as well as personal and pecuniary assistance, will be required; and it is hoped that whenever called upon to make an effort, every individual comprised in the general body of Manufacturers will be found ready and willing to tender his aid.

Whilst it affords a very sincere pleasure to the Committee to congratulate the general body of Manufacturers on the success which has hitherto attended their efforts, it is no less their grati-fication to acknowledge the confidence they have so long enjoyed, and should occasion again arise, as ere long it may, they will be again prepared to discharge their duty, and will endeavour to exercise the important functions confided to them with judgment and effect.

FINANCE.

It now only remains with the Committee to add a few words on the finances of the Association.

From the annexed statement it will appear that from 1838 to 1844, both inclusive, the sum of £1154. 14s. 9d. has been received and expended for the purposes of the Association, of which amount upwards of one half has been contributed by the Manchester Association.

The account shews that only the Manchester, Preston, and Burnley Associations have paid the full amount of the rates ordered by this Committee to be raised and paid to the general fund. The Committee are not disposed to believe that the absence of contributions denotes apathy, having had the satisfaction of witnessing evidence of local activity in places from whence they have derived no funds. It may however, be desirable, that parties so situated should consider whether in future they would not derive more advantage from a more thoroughly associated organization.

Doubtless, the present is a time requiring the greatest watchfulness and exertion to protect the interests of the trade, as well as to defend the characters of Mill Owners from the most unjust and unfounded calumny.

Although the Association has been enabled to effect much good with the funds at their disposal, your Committee have been compelled reluctantly to limit the efforts made to diffuse sound and correct views upon the subject of Factory Labour, and to promote the objects of the Association.

The Committee have to acknowledge the advantages which the Association, and the trade generally, have derived from the gratuitous personal efforts, and, it may be said, sacrifices of time and money which individuals have made in their untiring exertions to defend the interests and to establish the reputation of the trade, whenever they have found them assailed.

Nor ought they to omit to state, on this occasion, that not one of the gentlemen who have undertaken to appear upon deputations has received any payment for services rendered, and that in some instances they have not claimed any portion, and in other cases not the full amount, of the actual expenses which they have incurred.

It will be seen that the whole of the money raised has been already expended : the rules of the Association direct a rate to be laid so soon as the funds are reduced to £100.; and therefore it will be necessary at once to raise a further sum, for the purpose of defraying expenses which are now being incurred, as well as those which will, in all probability, attend the operations of the Association during the coming session of parliament.

Your Committee, relying upon the estimation of their previous efforts, on the part of the great body of the Manufacturers, appeal to them for their continued and increased support, in carrying out the objects of the Association. They entertain a strong opinion that the Manufacturers have only to act unitedly and with determination, in order to secure for themselves, in the minds of all candid men, their true position.

There can be no doubt, that the labours of the Association have already removed much of the prejudice, and triumphantly disposed of many of the unfounded statements put forth on the subject of Factory Labour; and your Committee entertain no doubt, that by united and determined action, any attempt at further legislative interference upon this subject during the next session of Parliament, will be successfully resisted, and that in all probability the renewal of such impolitic warfare will be indefinitely postponed.

On behalf of the Committee,

R. H. GREGG,

HENRY HOULDSWORTH,

JAMES MURRAY,

HENRY ASHWORTH,

LEWIS WILLIAMS,

THOMAS ASHTON,

DAVID HARRISON.

MANCHESTER,
Dec. 31st, 1844.

Dr. THE ASSOCIATION OF MILL OWNERS, IN ACCOUNT WITH J. MURRAY, Esq., TREASURER. **Cr.**

	£	s.	D.
1838 to 1844. To Salary of Secretary, at £50. per annum.	350	0	0
1837 to 1844. „ Postages, &c.	12	4	5
„ Printing and Stationery	127	16	0
1839 to 1844. „ Collecting Subscriptions	31	8	3
1844. „ Accountant making out Summaries of Returns, &c.	22	9	1
„ Various sums voted by the Central Committee, and expended in promoting the objects of the Association	180	0	0
„ Expenses of Deputations as follows:—			
1836 ..... £35 0 0			
1837 ..... 65 0 0			
1838 ..... 41 12 0			
1839 ..... 164 19 0			
1843 ..... 23 18 0			
1844 ..... 100 6 0	430	15	0
	£1154	**14**	**9**

		£	s.	D.
By Cash from T. Boothman, Junior		76	17	11
„ Cash from T. Boothman, Junior		22	18	0
„ Cash from Mr. Aaron Lees		30	12	8
„ Blackburn Local Association, 1838 ..... £21 17 0				
1841 ..... 10 0 0				
1843 ..... 20 0 0		51	17	0
„ Warrington Local Association, 1838 ..... 6 3 0				
1844 ..... 8 5 0		14	8	0
„ Preston Local Association, 1838 ..... 35 0 0				
1841 ..... 17 10 0				
1843 ..... 35 0 0				
1844 ..... 35 0 0		122	10	0
„ Bury Local Association, 1838 ..... 15 0 0				
„ Burnley Local Association, 1838 ..... 7 10 0				
1841 ..... 15 0 0				
1843 ..... 15 0 0				
1844 ..... 18 0 0		27	4	0
„ Stockport Local Association, 1838		55	10	0
„ Heywood Local Association, 1838 ..... 23 11 6				
1844 ..... 20 0 0		50	0	0
„ Ashton-under-Lyne Local Association, 1838 ..... 27 8 6				
1841 ..... 13 14 3				
1843 ..... 27 8 6		45	11	6
„ Manchester Association, 1838 ..... 159 12 3				
1841 ..... 48 1 5				
1843 ..... 87 0 0				
1844 ..... 244 14 0		68	11	3
„ Stalybridge Local Association, 1841		539	7	8
„ Interest from Bank, from 1839, to June 30th, 1844		21	0	0
„ Balance		26	13	4
		1	13	5
		£1154	**14**	**9**

British Labour Struggles:
Contemporary Pamphlets 1727-1850

An Arno Press/New York Times Collection

The Factory Act of 1833. 1833-1834.

Richard Oastler: King of Factory Children. 1835-1861.

The Battle for the Ten Hours Day Continues. 1837-1843.

The Factory Education Bill of 1843. 1843.

Prelude to Victory of the Ten Hours Movement. 1844.

Sunday Work. 1794-1856.

Demands for Early Closing Hours. 1843.

Conditions of Work and Living: The Reawakening of the English Conscience. 1838-1844.

Improving the Lot of the Chimney Sweeps. 1785-1840.

The Rising of the Agricultural Labourers. 1830-1831.

The Aftermath of the "Lost Labourers' Revolt". 1830-1831.